The Leadership Workout

PEARSON

At Pearson, we believe in learning – all kinds of learning for all kinds of people. Whether it's at home, in the classroom or in the workplace, learning is the key to improving our life chances.

That's why we're working with leading authors to bring you the latest thinking and best practices, so you can get better at the things that are important to you. You can learn on the page or on the move, and with content that's always crafted to help you understand quickly and apply what you've learned.

If you want to upgrade your personal skills or accelerate your career, become a more effective leader or more powerful communicator, discover new opportunities or simply find more inspiration, we can help you make progress in your work and life.

Pearson is the world's leading learning company. Our portfolio includes the Financial Times and our education business, Pearson International.

Every day our work helps learning flourish, and wherever learning flourishes, so do people.

To learn more, please visit us at **www.pearson.com/uk**

The Leadership Workout

The 10 tried-and-tested steps that will build your skills as a leader

Nick Winston

PEARSON

Harlow, England • London • New York • Boston • San Francisco • Toronto • Sydney
Auckland • Singapore • Hong Kong • Tokyo • Seoul • Taipei • New Delhi
Cape Town • São Paulo • Mexico City • Madrid • Amsterdam • Munich • Paris • Milan

Pearson Education Limited
Edinburgh Gate
Harlow CM20 2JE
United Kingdom
Tel: +44 (0)1279 623623
Web: www.pearson.com/uk

First published 2015 (print and electronic)

© Pearson Education Limited 2015 (print and electronic)

The right of Nick Winston to be identified as author of this work has been asserted by him in accordance with the Copyright, Designs and Patents Act 1988.

Pearson Education is not responsible for the content of third-party internet sites.

ISBN: 978-1-292-01771-6 (print)
   978-1-292-01773-0 (PDF)
   978-1-292-01774-7 (ePub)
   978-1-292-01772-3 (eText)

British Library Cataloguing-in-Publication Data
A catalogue record for the print edition is available from the British Library

Library of Congress Cataloging-in-Publication Data
Winston, Nick.
  The leadership workout : the 10 tried-and-tested steps that will build your
    skills as a leader / Nick Winston. — 1st Edition.
  pages cm
  ISBN 978-1-292-01771-6
  1. Leadership. I. Title.
  HD57.7.W56 2015
  658.4'092–dc23

                                                          201502442

10 9 8 7 6 5 4 3 2 1
19 18 17 16 15

Cover design by Two Associates
Print edition typeset in 10/13 Scene Std by 71
Print edition printed in Great Britain by Henry Ling Ltd, at the Dorset Press, Dorchester, Dorset

NOTE THAT ANY PAGE CROSS REFERENCES REFER TO THE PRINT EDITION

Contents

team, a happy boss and some semblance of a work/life balance!

Contents

Putting it into action (the mentor toolkit)   197

How to work with a manager, mentor or colleague
to put your new skills into action

Self-assessment questionnaire   201

What have you learnt?
What can you put into practice today?
How will you do it?

About the author

Nick Winston has over 20 years' experience as a leader and has spent the last 10 years as a consultant specialising in management and leadership development. In his previous roles, such as Managing Director of a recruitment consultancy and Training Manager for a Business Consultancy, Nick lead project teams of over 300 staff and acted as Lead Facilitator for some of Europe's largest Change and Transformation projects.

Nick has recently become an independent leadership consultant and trainer and is taking a part-time MSc in Business Psychology.

As well as consultancy and training delivery, Nick delivers interactive leadership sessions focused around Choice Architecture, Decision Theory, Problem Solving and Risk Perception.

Author's acknowledgements

Very few of the insights in this book have been my own. Most of the tools and techniques have been discovered and then rediscovered many times throughout history. They were originally brought to my attention by other consultants (and often course attendees) who felt strongly — as I do, that knowledge should be shared. So I would like to thank all of my colleagues, staff, clients and delegates who have been both teachers and sounding boards as well as willing guinea pigs at different times.

The tools and methods I have selected for this book have all been tested thoroughly over a period of years by colleagues, assorted business leaders and newly appointed leaders. They have been refined by constant feedback and tested in everyday real situations. They work. But picking the 10 most important tools for this book, from a list already whittled down to 20, was not easy. For help with this I would like to thank a few particular individuals, who patiently and expertly debated the value of each technique until we arrived at and agreed a top 10. Thanks to Feras, Emma, Matt, Emily, Tracey and Sandy for being part of this process over the last few years, for helping me to test these tools (sometimes in quite extreme conditions), and double-check their validity.

Finally I would like to give recognition to some people that I have never met, but whose ideas, research and writing have had a profound effect on my career and life; Daniel Kahneman and his colleagues Amos Tversky and Paul Slovic. I believe their research on decision theory and what Daniel later referenced as fast and slow thinking; will eventually become known as one of the most important theories for human progress and development. Only by understanding how we think can we stand a chance of successfully and positively changing our behaviour as a species.

Many thanks to everyone involved.

Publisher's acknowledgements

We are grateful to the following for permission to reproduce copyright material:

Figures

Figure on page 3 based on figure from Tannenbaum, A.S. and Schmitt, W.H., 1958. How to choose a leadership pattern. *Harvard Business Review,* 36, March–April, 95–101.

Picture credits

The publisher would like to thank the following for their kind permission to reproduce their photographs:

Alamy Images: dieKleinert page 148; Stanley Milgram with the shock machine. By permission of Alexandra Milgram: page 140; Subject pressing lever. From the film 'Obedience' by Stanley Milgram © 1968. Distributed by Alexander Street Press. By permission of Alexandra Milgram: page 142; **Getty Images:** Central Press/ Hulton Archive page 20; **Shutterstock.com**: Sarah Holmlund page 169.

All other images © Pearson Education

Every effort has been made to trace the copyright holders and we apologise in advance for any unintentional omissions. We would be pleased to insert the appropriate acknowledgement in any subsequent edition of this publication.

In some instances we have been unable to trace the owners of copyright material, and we would appreciate any information that would enable us to do so.

Introduction

In the early 1990s, one of the largest studies of 'why new leaders fail' took place in America. The research focused on well-educated, hardworking and motivated staff who had been promoted because of their high performance and positive attitude in their previous roles. **Hopefully, I have just described you!**

Failure was classed as: 'Did not deliver results expected', 'Took prolonged sick leave or ultimately left the role because of work-related stress', 'Was dismissed due to inappropriate actions such as a failure to comply with regulations, gross incompetence or actions that endangered others'.

Whilst I am sure these three points do not describe you, they are the very real outcomes for leaders and managers who do not know how to manage or lead.

The three main reasons for failure were identified as follows:

- Third biggest reason: **promoted because of previous knowledge and skill, but not given management or leadership training for new role.** People are promoted to a management position because they are good at their old jobs, but are not given adequate training for the job of being a manager or leader. **This is sometimes known as being promoted to a position of incompetence.**
- Second biggest reason: **doing the wrong thing.** Typically, this meant people were still trying to do their old roles whilst ignoring the need to actively manage and lead others. However, it also meant being unaware of organisational priorities and working on team tasks that were **not** important, whilst not finding time for tasks that actually **were** important.

Interestingly, later studies have shown that this is unlikely to be intentional, and is due to poor communication between the new leader and their senior line manager, leading to a lack of clarity about which tasks should be focused on.

- The single biggest reason for a new manager or leader failing was: (... if you can imagine a drum roll here, please...) **Felt unable to say no.**

If these three reasons sound familiar to you, then do not worry, help is at hand. This Business Gym workout will help you develop the skills and confidence you need to be an effective manager and leader. Whether you lead 1 person or 1,000, it will help you avoid the three biggest causes of failure for hard-working managers and leaders and, ultimately, make your life a lot easier as a result.

Whether you have been a manager for 15 days or 15 years, this book will help you. Your workout sessions will boost both your skills and confidence by exploring the 10 most effective and powerful steps for management and leadership.

This book has been designed to be used in three different ways:

1. You can simply dive into the relevant chapter that meets your current need.

2. You can work through the book from cover to cover and, in doing so, train yourself, using the explanations and exercises I have included for you.

3. You can create a learning group with your peers and use the book as a full learning programme – this is the most recommended option.

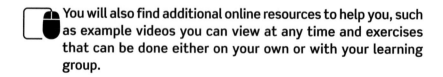 **You will also find additional online resources to help you, such as example videos you can view at any time and exercises that can be done either on your own or with your learning group.**

Icons will guide you as you move through each of the Business Gym workouts (steps) and each workout will follow the same structure, so your path to excellence will become familiar and easy.

You'll notice icons used in each chapter highlighting either an **Activity** (exercises for you to do by yourself or with your learning group), what we regard as a **Key idea** or **Media** (free additional resources available online at **www.thebusinessgym.net**). The icons are:

Activity   **Key idea**   **Media**

For the next few weeks, I will be your coach and trainer. And, like any good training regime at the gym, your workout sessions will have a structure. Each of the 10 steps (or workouts) is presented in the following way:

1. **Case study (Part 1: Example situation)** This is an initial description of the problem or situation in which you find yourself at work. You will be able to relate to these and they will help you define clearly what skill the step or session is focused on improving.

2. **Self-reflection** Here I will prompt you to think about your own practical examples of the situation. You will be asked questions such as, 'How much time is being wasted because of this issue?', 'What is the personal cost of having this problem unresolved?' and 'How would you like to be able to manage this situation in the future?' Just like at the gym, this part of the workout will help you focus on your goals and what you want to get out of the session.

3. **Tool or model** At this stage I will introduce you to the technique, a method or tool that is going to help you overcome your challenges and reach your goal. I have used hundreds of different techniques in my career as a management/leadership trainer and executive coach and I have chosen the 10 methods in this book very carefully.

   I have not selected the tools based on how original, well-known, modern or traditional they are. I have selected them based on only one criterion – **how well they work** in the real world.

4. **Case study (Part 2: How the example situation was resolved)** Examples build understanding so, before we explore how the

tool can help you, I will share with you how it helped someone in a very similar situation.

5. **Exercise: How to use this tool in your own situation** For each management tool, I will set you some questions or a framework exercise to help you learn and plan how to use the tool to manage your own situation.

6. **Call to action** Any good trainer or coach helps to keep their client motivated and energised, ready to take on the challenges that face them when they get back to work. Here I will pose some more motivating questions (that come from my executive coaching background):

   - What do you need to do?

   - What might stop you doing this?

   - How can you overcome that?

   - What might happen if you do not use the tool or model (i.e. do nothing)?

   - What will be the benefit or reward if you are able to use this tool?

   - How much time will you save over the next year by not having to constantly deal with this problem?

7. **In one sentence** Each workout session or lesson finishes with a statement or quote, designed to help the lesson stick in your mind.

First things first

As anyone who has ever joined a gym knows, normally, the first thing that you will do is an assessment of your current state of fitness and strength. This helps the trainer and gym member get a baseline against which to measure success and it also helps to highlight what exercises should be focused on and prioritised.

Whilst it still shocks me that this does not happen in the majority of professional management training courses, it is a great habit to get into and so, on the next page, you will find your pre-workout assessment.

A note to learning and development professionals and management trainers here: it will greatly improve the results of training programmes that you run, if you are able to get a baseline before the training begins. If done correctly, this will also form a critical part of your training needs analysis.

Self-assessment questionnaire

Complete the following questionnaire before you begin the book. Remember, this is not a test or an exam. It is simply a reflective assessment exercise to help give you a baseline for your existing knowledge, skill and confidence as a manager and leader of others. You do not have to share this with anyone, if you do not want to, although, if you are working through this book with a group of peers, you may find it very useful to share your results with each other. This will enable you to support each other better and utilise each other's strengths and experience in certain areas.

Score yourself on a scale of 1 to 10 for each of these questions, with 10 indicating a high level of confidence and skill and 1 the lowest.

1. How would you currently rate your **general management and leadership** skills? (How many hours a week do you spend currently worrying over whether you have managed a team member or situation correctly?)

2. How effective is your **communication**? (How many hours a week do you spend currently having the same conversation repeatedly because it was not understood or did not work the first time?)

3. How much are you **trusted** by your team? (How many hours a week do you spend currently trying to get people to trust you, for example, getting staff to be completely open and honest with you?)

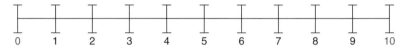

4. Do you currently **adapt your leadership style** for different people in different situations? (How many hours a week do you spend currently fixing your team members' mistakes or finding yourself exasperated or frustrated with one or more team members?)

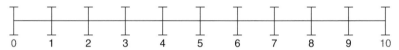

5. How good are you at **setting objectives** that meet your boss's requirements and are met by your team? (How many hours a week do you spend currently chasing team members' objectives/results or putting in fixes because an objective has not been met?)

6. How comfortable or confident are you in **delegating** work to your team? (How many hours a week do you spend currently doing work that deep down you know you should delegate but do not feel that you can?)

7. How good are you at **motivating** others? How engaged and motivated is your team? (How many hours a week do you

spend currently trying to motivate people, particularly the person who is really difficult to motivate?)

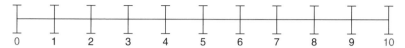

8. How comfortable or confident are you in giving constructive **feedback** that actually leads to improvements? (How many hours a week do you spend currently worrying about or avoiding giving difficult feedback or giving the same feedback multiple times because the first time it was not taken on board?)

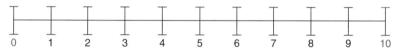

9. Do you feel that you are more **reactive** (1) or **proactive** (10) in your work as a manager? (How many hours a week do you spend currently reacting to situations and putting out fires instead of planning in order to ensure that problems do not happen in the first place?)

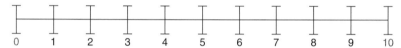

10. How comfortable are you in **managing upwards** and saying no to your own line manager? (How many hours a week do you spend currently achieving the unachievable, working without the correct resourcing levels or worrying about how to manage your manager?)

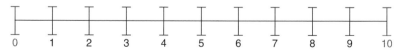

These are your baselines. Undoubtedly, you will want to check how they have improved when you get to the end of this learning programme, which is why the post-workout assessment is at the end of the book. Each question in this questionnaire is related to one of the steps, so, if you have identified one particular area that you really feel you would like to develop first, you may choose to jump straight to the relevant step. For example, if you are scoring 8+ on everything except managing upwards, you might first want to work through **Step 10**: Managing up.

10 steps to better leadership

The difference between management and leadership and how both can be learned.

Step 1   Developing the right attitude

Step 2   Communication – how to get the best out of people

Step 3   How to build trust

Step 4   Adapting your leadership style for the best outcome

Step 5   Setting objectives that work

Step 6   Delegating to and up-skilling your team

Step 7   Motivating and engaging people

Step 8   Giving feedback that leads to positive change

Step 9   Moving from being reactive to proactive

Step 10   Managing up (or how to say no without ruining your career)

Before I begin a management or leadership training programme, I find it very useful to clarify the answers to two simple, but powerful, questions.

1 What is the difference between leadership and management?

2 Do you have to be born a leader or is leadership a skill that can be learned?

Before we look at the answers to these questions, try and answer them either by yourself or with your learning group. The table below will help you clarify your thoughts around the first question.

 **Exercise**

What are the roles and duties of a manager?	What are the roles and duties of a leader?
Write your answers here:	Write your answers here:

The answer is that a manager is concerned primarily with getting things done. This includes the allocation of duties, tasks and resources. A leader is concerned primarily with a longer-term strategic view of what should get done and then concerned with inspiring people to get that done.

You might say that a manager looks after the nuts and bolts of the systems and processes, whereas a leader looks at the long-term view and tends to the fluffier side of things, often using words such as engagement and vision.

This then begs the question, where does being a manager stop and being a leader start?

Groups that I have worked with have come to one clear conclusion on this time after time:

There is not a clear split or single point at which everything changes.

 A manager or leader is someone who has to manage and lead others. As soon as you are promoted to a supervisory role, you need to be both!

To be a really good manager you will need to lead people and to be a really good leader you will need to understand and manage resources, processes and systems.

As early as 1973, Robert Tannenbaum and Warren H. Schmidt recognised that the move from manager to leader was more of a gradual change than a defined split. They created a (now famous) diagram, which showed that being a manager and being a leader are not two separate things, although the focus does change as you progress up the company hierarchy (see the following figure).

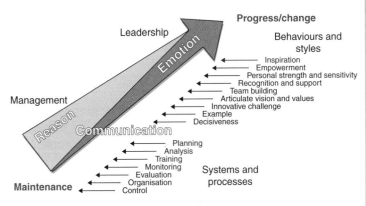

Tannenbaum and Schmidt's leadership model

Now let us look at that second big question:

Do you have to been born a leader or is leadership a skill that can be learned?

Whilst it is true that some people find it easier to lead than others, it is not an innate skill. There will always be a natural leader in a group (normally the most confident and supportive person). However, leadership is like any other skill and follows a classical model for how it can be learned and developed.

When you are first thrust into a management position, you may have little idea of what is required in order to lead a team. In the model of learning figure, shown on the next page, this is referred to as **unconscious incompetence,** i.e. you are not even aware (unconscious) what you do not know (incompetence).

When you start to experience difficulties as a manager or leader, you realise quickly that you need to learn some new skills. This is referred to as **conscious incompetence,** i.e. you are now aware (conscious) of where the holes in your knowledge are (incompetence).

Eventually, through experience, training or luck, you learn some key leadership and management skills. At this stage, they do not come naturally to you and you need to focus, or be very deliberate (conscious) when you use them. This is referred to as the **conscious competence** phase, i.e. you can do it, but you really have to focus on it consciously to do it well.

Finally, with enough practice, the skills become second nature. This phase is called **unconscious competence,** i.e. you can do it so well (competence) that you are not even aware of doing it (unconscious).

 The great news, then, is that not only can anyone learn to be a good manager or leader, but that, with enough practice, it can become second nature!

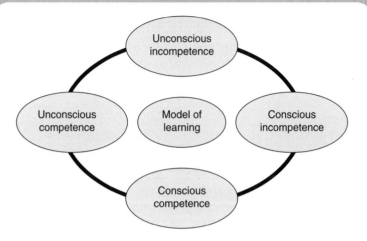

Model of learning

The model of learning above is a great description of how you learn almost any skill. It is worth noting that it is a continuous cycle. For example, at what stage of the cycle would I be if I started to drive in extremely icy conditions in Scandinavia? Although I might consider myself a generally competent driver, it is likely that I would be back at stage 1, unconscious incompetence, until I got some ice driving lessons and experience.

 There is no harm in recognising when you are unconsciously incompetent for a new skill (such as leadership). In fact, it can be one of the most beneficial realisations that you can have.

 You can view a podcast that summarises the main points of this part at:

www.thebusinessgym.net

Step 1

Developing the right attitude

After reading this step you will:

- Have a point of reference for good leadership in any situation
- Have a way to decide instantly what the right course of action should be in any leadership situation.

Case study

Part 1: Example situation

You have a leadership issue (let us pick something typical, such as your department is going through yet another reorganisation!). But, also, you seem to have a thousand other things to do as well as various deadlines to meet and a veritable host of urgent issues. How can you get a quick answer to 'how to manage your leadership issue', without ploughing through all the notes from your leadership courses?

Many thousands of books have been written about management and leadership and the type of manager or leader an individual can be. Managers and leaders can be autocratic, democratic, authoritarian, enabling, supportive, controlling, task-focused, team-focused, visible, absent, micromanaging, macro-focused, people managers, strategic managers, etc.

In this step we will look at just two types of manager/leader: good ones and bad ones.

1 Good managers/leaders are successful. They are individuals who are effective and efficient. They communicate clearly, get the task completed, get the best out of their people and are not over stressed.

2 Bad managers/leaders are less successful. They are individuals who are not effective and not as efficient. Often, they fail to communicate clearly, have difficulty completing tasks, fail to get the best out of their people and are in a state of extreme stress.

Unfortunately, worrying about what to do in each different leadership situation can sap strength and energy. Also, it can lead to something called paralysis through analysis, i.e. you spend so long worrying about what you should do, you delay actually doing it, which, in turn, often makes the situation worse!

Self-reflection

- How much management or leadership training have you had in your role so far?
- How many hours per week do you spend currently worrying about whether you are a good manager or leader or what you should do in certain management and leadership situations?

You may want to take a moment to note down some of the situations you are thinking of.

Tool or model

The first tool to consider in this book's 10 steps is also, perhaps, the most important. It has been many years since I have run a management or leadership training session that did not start with this tool and it has become one of my all-time favourites.

What you are about to find out is that you already know what to do in almost any management situation.

 Exercise

Think of the best and worst managers or leaders that you have ever had or met.

- Note down their attributes.
- Then note down how that affected you as a staff/team member. (If you were not part of their team, how do you think their way of managing affected the team?)

Best manager/leader ever	Worst manager/leader ever
Write down 20 words to describe their actions or attributes:	Write down 20 words to describe their actions or attributes:
Write down 20 words to describe how that affected how their team felt and acted:	Write down 20 words to describe how that affected how their team felt and acted:

Now consider the next few questions.

- For which manager or leader were you most productive and effective? Or which individual had the most productive and effective team? (Do not confuse hours worked with productivity and effectiveness. Often, you find that people will work longer hours for the worst manager out of fear. However, because they have clearer directions, feel valued and engaged, they are far more productive and effective for the good manager.)
- Given the productivity of their teams, which individual do you think had the easier life?
- Which manager or leader seemed to be happiest?
- Which person was respected more within the organisation?

Did you know that, in a study of over 2,000 civil servants, it was found that if staff described their manager as good and supportive, that manager was likely to live, on average, two years longer after retirement than a manager who was described as bad and uncaring!

Case study

Part 2: How the example situation was resolved

As you can see, there is an easy way to decide how to manage or lead in almost any situation. Anyone faced with a new situation simply need ask themselves:

'What would the good manager or leader do here? What would the bad manager or leader do here?'

In the example described at the start of this step (the reorganisation during a very busy period), the good manager

My task list

Importance/priority	Task
1st	Push back on non-urgent deadline to enable time for departmental meeting.
2nd	Departmental meeting about reorganisation. Check everyone knows why it is happening and gather ideas from team for how to do it with minimal disruption.
3rd	Communicate with stakeholders to manage expectations during period of change.

would reprioritise their task list. Near the top of list would be sitting down with the department and explaining why the reorganisation was happening, discussing how it would impact everyone and creating a joint plan for how to minimise disruption.

The good leader puts their team first because that is how they keep morale and engagement high and get the team to deliver the greatest productivity.

The bad manager would avoid dealing with the situation or, perhaps, simply command everyone to get on with it and stop whining about it. This would lead to decreased morale and engagement and, ultimately, harm productivity.

By following the actions of the good manager and ensuring that they do not follow the actions of the bad manager, an individual generally can manage any situation without having to read the 1,000+ books on management and leadership.

This lesson has been invaluable in my own management and leadership career.

Many times I felt like I wanted to sack someone, shout at them (more so in my early career than in the last 15 years), or avoid dealing with a situation completely because I felt it might blow up in my face.

However, before doing what my emotions and the stress of the situation were encouraging me to do, I asked myself, 'What would the best manager I know do?' and 'What would the worst manager I know do?' The answers were instantaneous and obvious. And, even if the answer was not what I secretly hoped it would be (for example, do not avoid the issue, tackle it), I knew deep down the answer was right.

Should I shout at the person who was underperforming? No, I should find out why they were underperforming so together we can fix it.

Should I avoid performance managing the slacker in the team who used a wheelchair and accused anyone who tried to manage her performance of bullying and discrimination? No, I should tackle the situation in a respectful but direct manner. Why? Because this is what the good manager would do and, therefore, it was always the best thing in the long run, both for me, my team, my company **and** the individual who was presenting me with a difficult situation.

 Exercise

How to use this tool in your own situation

So, which column would you like to fit into as a manager/leader?

The best mangers and leaders:

- support their staff
- give clear instructions
- give recognition when it is deserved
- challenge and develop their staff without overloading or breaking them
- listen
- make people feel valued
- get a better standard of work out of people
- get higher productivity and initiative from their staff
- have highly successful teams.

In order to check that you are one of the good ones, what words do you want your staff to use to describe your management and leadership style?

Words I would like my staff to use when describing my management and leadership style:

Keep a copy of this handy, making sure it is visible during most of the day. Take a picture and print it, or type it out in a PDF or Word document and then print it. Alternatively, transfer the results to whiteboard, flipchart, tablet, laptop, PC or window where they will be visible.

Here is the really good news.

No matter what difficult leadership situations your working life throws at you, you actually already know the answer. Ensure that this table is locked into your brain; it is one of the most important tools for management and leadership you will ever come across. Next time you find yourself in a leadership situation and you are unsure how to handle it, just think, 'What would the good manager/leader do? What would the bad manager/leader do?' and you will have your answer.

As you progress through the rest of this book, you will see that the tools covered are used by the good manager/leader and not the bad manager/leader.

I will finish off this step with some points to support this learning.

Exercise

Take a moment to consider why the bad manager was acting the way they did.

Were they born evil? Or was something else going on? Could there be a reason for their behaviour?

If you are like the majority of junior, middle and senior managers that I have worked with over the last 15 years, then you will have come up with the following answers:

- The bad manager was metaphorically drowning, they could not do their job, and they were incompetent.
- They had a really bad manager themselves (a learned behaviour pattern).
- They probably did not understand the impact of their actions on their team and therefore on themselves.
- They had not been trained well.

So, next time you see a really bad manager or leader, do not be angry at them, feel sorry for them. They are likely to be highly stressed because they are not coping. They will be angry at the world, have a hard-working but unproductive team and they are, statistically, likely to die two years earlier than their good manager counterparts.

You already know how to be a good manager or leader. You also know that pressure at work can push you towards being a bad manager or leader. It is important to recognise when this is happening. By actively focusing on these skills, you can increase our own management and leadership abilities simply by asking yourself, 'What would the best manager or leader do or say in this situation?'

Never be afraid to reflect on this question; it will help protect you and keep you on the path of good leadership and a long and happy life!

 Now you know that you already knew the secret to being a great leader, how much less time will you spend worrying about what to do instead of just doing it?

Call to action

Answer the following questions honestly. If you are working with a learning group, then share the answers.

- Based on what you have explored in this step, what do you need to do to be a successful manager/leader?
- What might stop you doing this?
- How can you overcome that?
- What might happen if you do not use this tool or model (i.e. do nothing)?
- What will be the benefit or reward if you are able to use this tool?
- How much time will you save over the next year by not overly worrying about what you should be doing in management situations?

In one sentence

What would the good manager do, what would the bad manager do, therefore what will I do?

 You can view a podcast that summarises the main points of this step at:

www.thebusinessgym.net

Step 2

Communication – how to get the best out of people

After reading this step you will:

- Understand how to adapt your communication style for different people in order to maximise engagement

- Be able to communicate in a clearer and more effective manner with different types of people

- Know a little bit more about what motivates you and the people you are working with

- Be able to avoid a lot of the miscommunication and conflict that normally happens in everyday life.

Case study

Part 1: Example situation

You have just asked someone to do something for the third time and either they have not done it, or they have done it the wrong way! This is frustrating for everyone involved.

Another related situation is trying to engage someone, who is not a direct report, to help achieve a task and being unable to get them to do it.

Both types of failure waste a lot of resources (time) and, in doing so, add to the time pressures on the leader. These situations are related because they are both about effective communication. When it comes to communicating, success depends both on what you say and how you say it. So, how can you ensure that communication is effective? That is, how can you communicate in a way that is most likely to achieve someone doing something for you and getting it right the first time?

I started my first company at the age of 21. By the time I was 22, I had nearly destroyed it. With hindsight, I later understood that it was because of how I spoke to people. You see, I firmly believed in the following statement:

> 'You should speak to people in the way in which you would like to be spoken to.'

Perhaps you completely agree with this statement. I find that many decent and intelligent people do, but let me share with you what this meant in practice.

At the age of 21 I was a very confident person. I earned more money than any of my friends and peers, I was highly competitive, extremely direct, thick skinned, blunt in my language and, let's be frank, quite cocky and arrogant as well. Therefore, when I spoke to people in the way in which I would like to be spoken to, it was in a very direct and challenging way. I did not use words such as please and thank you much, because I did not appreciate them when they were said to me. (I felt they were unnecessary and weak.) If you are thinking, 'Well, that's just rude', you are probably correct; it was rude, but it is **how I liked to be spoken to.**

If you wanted to get me to do something, then the wrong way was to be really nice about it, explain how you would support me and add lots of pleases. If you spoke to me that way, I would quickly become bored, disengaged and, ultimately, frustrated with you. The successful way to get me to do something was to be brief and direct, tell me it was difficult and that I probably could not do it! That is, challenge me and make it interesting. So, I spoke to people in the way in which I liked to be spoken to – in that challenging and direct manner. I am sure it will not surprise you to read that only a few people in my team responded well to this. These were the people who had a similar communication style as me. Unfortunately, the majority of my employees had a very different style of communication and, therefore, really did not appreciate my brisk tone.

Generally, I found the whole situation very frustrating. Often, I would make people upset or completely disengage them, when actually I was trying to encourage and engage them. Often, I found myself walking away from a conversation thinking, 'What the hell happened there?', 'Why on earth did they react like that?' or 'This person just wants to be difficult.'

In my career as a management trainer and consultant, I have also witnessed variations on this problem many times: managers who approach others in a very soft and polite way but are met with indifference, disdain and viewed as weak; managers who are very enthusiastic and jolly in their communication approach but who are viewed by the analysts who work for them as idiots who lack detail; managers who are technical, precise and detail oriented in their communication and who are viewed as lacking charisma and quickly bore some of their staff to a point of complete disengagement. We all have different ways of communicating. If you can understand how the other person prefers to be communicated with, you can be far more successful in influencing, delegating and engaging them with what needs to be done.

Self-reflection

- How do you speak to people? How do you like to be spoken to? Does everyone else in your team speak in the same way?
- How do you think your stakeholders like to be spoken to?
- Who speaks to you in a way that just irritates you? Are there people to whom you speak who you just do not seem to get on with?
- How much time have you wasted having repeated conversations about the same thing because the communication clearly did not work the first time?
- How much time do you spend currently in conversations that clearly are a waste of time for both parties?
- What would the result be if you could tune in to the other person's way of communicating?

 **Exercise**

Try filling in the table below to identify some of the more severe problems with communication. You will learn how to overcome these problems later in this step.

Who do you have particularly bad communication with?	
What, specifically, do they do in the conversation that negatively impacts the outcome?	
What, specifically, do **you** do in the conversation that seems to annoy the other person and negatively impacts the outcome?	

Tool or model

A couple of millennia ago the ancient Greeks wrote that people have different personalities, different motivators and different ways of communicating. This is an idea that has been played with a lot over the centuries and, in the last hundred years or so, psychologists such as Carl Jung, Abraham Maslow and Carl Rogers refined the idea a little more. Jung, in particular, realised that, by paying attention to how people speak, we can get an insight into what makes them tick, what their motivators are and how we can engage them in a task, idea or project. This is at the heart of influencing skills and good communication.

Carl Gustav Jung, often referred to as C. G. Jung, was a Swiss psychiatrist and psychotherapist who founded analytical psychology. Jung proposed and developed the concepts of extraversion and introversion, archetypes, and the collective unconscious.

Building on the work of these psychologists, there are now many different tools and systems that help people to realise what their own personality and communication style is (already you may have come across MBTI, Insights, SDI, FIRO-B, PQR-32, Prism, Hogan's 360, etc.).

In this step we will look at a tool that will help you to recognise quickly not just your own style, but also the preferred style of other people. By being aware of both your own natural communication style and the other person's preferred style, you can increase drastically the effectiveness of communication and your ability to manage, engage, influence and motivate others.

Feedback over hundreds of leadership courses from literally thousands of delegates has shown that these categorising frameworks are one of the most valuable tools for any leader.

 This step will use a categorising tool called the combined reflective tool (CRT). Go to www.thebusinessgym.net to access a reflective questionnaire that can help you pinpoint your own style. One of the great things about this system is that it is intuitive. Simply by reading the descriptions that follow, you will get a good idea of who you are and how you communicate. This will not only show you how you like to be communicated with, it will also reveal to you how you may have been communicating in completely the wrong way with that difficult person who you just cannot seem to connect with.

The four styles are **friend, socialite, challenger** and **expert** (see the following figure).

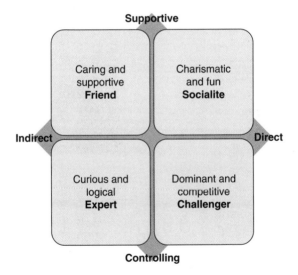

Whilst it is true that every human has a little bit of each style in them, we all have a strong preference for one type of style. Normally, we find it easy to get along with the two other styles that sit either side of us (see the figure above) and very difficult to communicate with the remaining style that sits opposite us in this figure.

Here is a very brief summary of the four styles.

Style	Motivators (what is important to them)	Demotivators (what they do not like and actively will avoid)	How they judge themselves and others	How they like to be communicated with
Friend Supportive, indirect, caring and kind	• Being nice • Being kind • Helping others • Being in a team • Politeness • Consideration for others • Emotion • Openness	• Conflict • Competitiveness • Arrogance (over confidence) • Lack of manners	**Am I.../Are you...** • Supportive • Considerate • Kind • Nice	Polite but friendly and informal. A calm and supportive (soft) manner should be used at all times. Always use please and thank you.
Socialite Fun, charismatic, direct, high energy	• Fun • Positivity • Being nice • Excitement • High energy • Concepts • Attention • Recognition • Openness	• Being ignored • Too much detail • Repetitive tasks • Boredom • Lack of recognition • Looking bad (foolish or stupid)	**Am I.../Are you...** • Liked • Sociable • Fun • Supportive • Confident • Charismatic • Well regarded • Complimentary	Friendly, informal and fun. Communicate enthusiastically and do not go into too much detail (it is boring). Compliments are important.

Style	Motivators (what is important to them)	Demotivators (what they do not like and actively will avoid)	How they judge themselves and others	How they like to be communicated with
Challenger Dominant, controlling, direct, competitive	• The challenge • Competition • Success • The result • Directness • Strength • Control • Tenacity • Willpower	• Emotional waffle • Weakness (fluffiness versus too much detail) • Pointless discussion • Lack of challenge (if it is easy, there is no point doing it!)	**Am I.../Are you...** • Successful • Competent • Capable • Strong • Resolute • Rising to the challenge • Direct • Confident	Be direct and challenging. Do not waffle. Do not worry about manners, just get straight to the point. Be confident.
Expert Controlling – indirect, analytical	• Intellectual challenge • Analysis • Understanding • Logical thought • Routes, systems and processes • Autonomy • Fairness • Justice • Expertise	• Lack of detail • Badly thought-out processes • Invasion of privacy • Faking knowledge • Lack of substance • Lack of clarity • Sacrificing thoroughness for speed	**Am I.../Are you...** • Intelligent • Correct • Competent • Calm • In control • Balanced • Judicious • Analytical • Expert	Be calm, polite (formal) and detailed. Communication should be backed by clear written instructions, where possible.

Having read the brief description of the four styles, you can probably already get an idea of which category (or categories) you fit into. You can also get a good idea of which categories the people you have unsuccessful communication with fit into.

Wherever you are, it is worth noting that you will have difficulty communicating with different styles to your own and, in particular, those opposite you in the grid (see the figure below).

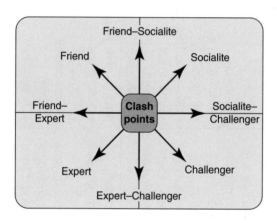

More detailed descriptions of the four main styles follow.

The friend (supportive/indirect)

The diplomatic friend is supporting and indirect, relatively unassertive, warm and reliable. Friends sometimes are seen by others as soft-hearted and acquiescent.

Friends seek security. They take action and make decisions slowly. This pace stems from their desire to avoid risky or unknown situations. Before they take action or make a decision, they need to know how other people feel about their decision.

Friends tend to be the most people-oriented of the four styles. Having close, friendly, personal and first-name relationships with people is one of their most important objectives. They dislike interpersonal conflict so much that sometimes they say what they think other people want to hear. They have natural counselling skills and are extremely supportive. Their motto is:

'Notice how nice a person I am!'

Friends tend to be good, active listeners and generally develop relationships with people who are good active listeners. As a result, friends have strong networks of people who are willing to be mutually supportive. Often, you feel good just being with a friend.

Friends focus on getting acquainted and building trust. They are irritated by pushy, aggressive behaviour. They question how things will affect their personal circumstances and camaraderie of the group. They are cooperative, steady workers and excellent team players.

The primary strengths of friends are relating to, caring for and loving others. Their primary weaknesses are that they are somewhat unassertive, overly sensitive and easily bullied.

Ideal occupations for the friend cluster around the helping professions, such as counselling, teaching, social work, the clergy, psychology, nursing, parenting and human resource development.

In the business environment, friends like others to be courteous, friendly and accepting of their share of the responsibility, and genuine.

Friends' desks contain family pictures and other personal items. Their office walls have personal slogans, family or group photos, serene pictures or mementos. Friends are high touch in a high-tech world. They give their offices a friendly, warm ambience and arrange seating in a side-by-side cooperative manner.

To achieve balance and behavioural flexibility, friends need to:

- say no occasionally
- attend to the completion of tasks without over-sensitivity to the feelings of others
- be willing to reach beyond their comfort zone to set goals that require some stretch and risk
- delegate to others.

Communicating with friends

Friendliness and politeness are important to friends. They like a calm, supportive approach and are motivated by helping others (supportive and indirect). They do not like what they see as uncaring, brisk and aggressive behaviour. The perfect way to delegate to a friend is:

> 'Would you please do this for me? I would very much appreciate it and, in doing this, you will really help the rest of the team. I have faith in you, but I want you to know that I will be here to support you and you can ask questions at any time.'

The socialite (supportive and direct)

Socialites are direct and supportive, exhibiting characteristics such as animation, intuitiveness and liveliness. But they can also be viewed as manipulative, impetuous and excitable when displaying behaviour inappropriate to a situation.

Socialites are fast paced. Their actions and decisions are spontaneous and are seldom concerned with facts and details; they try to avoid them as much as possible. Their motto is:

> 'Let's have fun! Do not confuse me with the facts.'

This disregard for details sometimes prompts them to exaggerate and generalise facts and figures. It also gives them a built-in excuse when they are wrong: 'I did not have all the facts!'. They are more comfortable with best guesstimates than with exact data.

Socialites' primary strengths are their enthusiasm, persuasiveness and delightful sociability. Their primary weaknesses are getting involved in too many things, impatience and their short attention spans, which cause them to become bored easily.

Socialites are ideas people. They have the ability to get others caught up in their dreams because of their good persuasive skills. They influence others and shape their environment by bringing others into alliance to accomplish results. They seek approval and recognition for their accomplishments and achievements and have a dynamic ability to think on their feet.

Socialites are true entertainers. They love the audience and thrive on involvement with people. They tend to work quickly and enthusiastically with others.

Socialites are stimulating, talkative and gregarious. They tend to operate on intuition and like to take risks. Their greatest irritations are boring tasks, being alone and not having access to a telephone.

Many socialites are in occupations such as sales, relationship management, entertainment, public relations, professional hosting, and can be lawyers, social directors on cruise ships, in the hotel business and other glamorous high-profile careers. In the business environment they like other people to be risk-takers and to act quickly, be uninhibited, spontaneous and entertaining.

Socialites design and use their space in a disorganised, creative and cluttered manner. Their walls may hold awards, stimulating posters or notes and motivational personal slogans. Their seating indicates warmth, openness and a willingness to make contact. Since socialites do not have issues with physical closeness and do not mind a slap on the back or a handshake, often they move to an alternative seating arrangement when talking with visitors. There is little danger of alienating socialites by standing too close or playing with something on their desks.

To achieve balance and behavioural flexibility, socialites need to:

- control their time and emotions
- develop a more objective mindset
- spend more time checking, verifying, specifying, organising and developing a greater task-focus
- take a more logical approach to projects and issues.

Communicating with socialites

Socialites can communicate effectively with both challengers and friends, as they are supportive and competitive. They find it difficult to communicate effectively with experts. Socialites perceive experts as boring, unsociable, aloof and too focused on detail, whilst experts perceive socialites as unfocused exaggerators – over the top and with no real focus. Socialites are (unsurprisingly) the most social of all the styles and they are engaged by communication with lots of enthusiasm and positive recognition. The best way to delegate to a socialite is to say something like:

> 'I would love for you to do this. It is an exciting project. It is a bit tricky but I absolutely think you will completely succeed with it because you are great at this sort of thing. Oh and, by the way, when you do succeed, which I know you will, I will make damn sure everyone knows what a great job you did.'

The challenger (controlling and direct)

Dominant challengers are controlling and direct. They exhibit firmness in their relationship with others, are orientated towards productivity and goals and are concerned with bottom-line results.

Challengers accept challenges, take authority and go head first into solving problems. They tend to exhibit great administrative and operational skills and work quickly and impressively on their own environment.

They tend to appear as cool, independent and competitive with others, especially in a business environment. Challengers try to shape their environment to overcome obstacles en route to their accomplishments. They demand maximum freedom to manage themselves and others and use their leadership skills to become winners.

Their weak traits include stubbornness, impatience and toughness. Challengers tend to take control of others and have a low tolerance of their feelings, attitudes and inadequacies with delays. It is not unusual for a challenger to call you and, without saying hello, launch right into the conversation: 'You've got to be kidding; the shipment from Hong Kong will kill us. . . by the way, this is Jack.'

When other people cannot keep up with their speed, they view them as incompetent. The challengers' motto might be:

> 'I want it done right and I want it done now' or 'I want it done yesterday!'

Challengers like to juggle three things at once and, when they feel comfortable with those three things, they pick up a fourth. They keep adding more until the pressure adds to the point where they let everything drop, then immediately start the whole process over again. The challengers' theme may be '**Notice my accomplishments.**' Their high-achievement motivation gives challengers a tendency towards workaholism.

Their strengths are their ability to get things done, their desire for leadership and their decision-making ability. Their weaknesses tend to be inflexibility, impatience, poor listening habits and failure to take time to smell the flowers.

In fact, they are so competitive, when they do finally go out to smell the flowers, they return and say to everyone else, 'I smelled 12 flowers today. How many did you smell?'

A challenger's ideal occupation might be a hard-driving stockbroker, independent consultant, corporate CEO, drill sergeant or monarch. In a business, they like others to be decisive, efficient, receptive, tough, intelligent, quick and assertive.

A challenger's desk will be busy with paperwork, projects and material separated in to piles. Their offices are decorated to suggest power. Challengers are formal and keep their distance physically and psychologically.

A stereotypical challenger's office is arranged so that seating is formal – face to face with a big power desk separating them from their visitors. They do not appreciate people talking three inches from their noses and will see it as a challenge (to which they will rise), so becoming your friend is not a prerequisite to doing business with you.

To achieve balance and behavioural flexibility, challengers need to:

- practise active listening
- pace themselves to look more relaxed
- develop patience, humility and sensitivity
- show concern for others
- use more caution
- verbalise the reasons for the conclusions
- participate more as team players.

Communicating with challengers

The competitive challengers are the opposite of friends. Challengers like concise communication, they love to challenge and be challenged, they do not like emotional waffle and, the more pleases and thank yous that you use, the more irritated and disengaged the challenger becomes. The perfect way to delegate to a challenger is:

'This is difficult; are you up for it?'

Challengers and friends do not get along naturally, with the challenger communication style seeming to be very aggressive to the friend and the friend's communication style perceived as wet or weak by the challenger.

The expert (controlling/indirect)

The analytical expert is both indirect and controlling. They are concerned with logical, well thought-out process and are persistent, systematic problem solvers. They can also be seen as aloof, picky and critical.

Experts are very security-conscious and have a strong need to be right, leading them to an over reliance on data collection. In their quest for data, they tend to ask many questions about specifics. Their actions and decisions tend to be slow and extremely cautious. Although they are great problem solvers, experts could be more decisive decision makers.

Experts tend to be perfectionists, serious and orderly. They focus on the details and the processes of work and become irritated by surprises and glitches. Their motto is:

'Notice my efficiency'

and their emphasis is on compliance and working within existing guidelines to promote quality in products and service.

Experts like organisation and structure and dislike too much involvement with other people. They work carefully and precisely by themselves, are time disciplined and prefer an intellectual work environment. Experts tend to be sceptical and critical of their own performance. They like to see things in writing.

Experts' primary strengths are their accuracy, dependability, independence, follow-through and organisation.

Their primary weaknesses are their procrastination and conservative natures, which promote their tendency to be picky and over-cautious.

Occupations that they tend to gravitate towards are accounting, engineering, computer programming, the hard sciences (chemistry, physics and maths), system analysis and architecture.

The greatest irritation for experts is disorganised, illogical people.

In business environments, they want others to be credible, competent, professional, courteous and sincere.

Experts tend to have highly organised desks. Paperwork may appear messy but it will be stacked in a logical order. The expert will know where everything is and notice if anything is missing.

Their office walls contain their favourite types of artwork: charts, graphs, exhibits or pictures pertaining to the job. Experts are non-contact people who prefer the formality of distance. This preference is reflected in the functional but uninviting arrangement of their desk and chairs. They are not fond of huggers and touchers and prefer a cool handshake.

To achieve balance and behavioural flexibility, experts need to:

- openly show concern and appreciation of others
- occasionally try shortcuts and time savers
- adjust more readily to change and disorganisation
- improve timely decision making and initiation of new projects
- compromise with the opposition
- state unpopular decisions
- use policies more as guidelines than hard and fast laws.

Communicating with experts

Experts love detail, accuracy and written communication, such as email. They like a calm approach and are, perhaps, the least social of all the styles. Experts love intellectual challenges and are naturally polite people (though often are seen as unnecessarily formal by socialites). Their desire to focus on the technical detail and not engage in pointless waffle can sometimes make them appear to be a little disengaged to the socialite, who the expert may view as a pointless incompetent and a waste of time. Experts and socialites do not get along naturally.

The best way to delegate to an expert is as follows:

> *'I have an interesting technical problem that seems to be a little tricky to solve. If I give you all of the information and leave you alone to have a look at it, could you give me your recommendations, please?'*

Case study

Part 2: How the example situation was resolved

Now let us go back to the situation I found myself in when I was a young man running my first company. I am sure you have realised the problem by now; I was a challenger and I was communicating with people who were not all challengers themselves. My direct and competitive (some might even say aggressive and confrontational) communication style worked well with the other challenger types in my company, but the experts and socialites did not particularly like it and the **friends** found it confusing, upsetting and very disengaging.

In order to communicate well with everyone in my company, first I had to understand who I was, and then think about how I could and should adapt my communication style for different people. For some, that meant being a little more friendly and complimentary (socialites); for others, I chose to speak in a calmer tone, ensuring I was always accurate, that I examined the details and focused on the process (experts); and, for the friends, I needed to make the biggest changes of all (because they were my opposite style). With friends, I started to make sure that I sat down with them, spoke calmly and in a friendly, informal manner, was polite, asked for things nicely and, most importantly, that I showed consideration for others.

Almost overnight, the engagement levels and subsequent performance of all of my staff increased, even with the two challenger types for whom I did not need to adapt my communication style. Better communication led to a happy group of people which, in turn, led to a more successful company.

It is important to note that I adapted my communication style, but I did not fake it or pretend to be someone I was not. As a leader, it is important to be authentic or genuine. The people around you will quickly be able to tell if you are manipulating them and being false instead of just respecting their style of communication and adapting to it. I did not pretend to be a friend, expert or socialite, but then I did not need to. As I started to speak partially in their style of communication, amazingly they started to reflect mine! The friends became more assertive around me (perhaps because they were less worried about whether I would shout at them), the experts got to the point more quickly and would happily summarise things for me (perhaps because they had more confidence in me and did not think I needed everything spelling out for me any more) and the socialites started to understand that I truly did value them, which led to long-lasting benefits for everyone concerned.

I continued doing this and something else both unexpected and positive happened. As I stepped into the world of others and used more friend, expert and socialite communication styles, I started to understand a little more of what motivated my staff: when delegating to **friends,** I would discuss the benefits to everyone, if they would kindly help me with the task; I would challenge the experts' intellect and problem-solving skills (always in a calm and considerate way); and I would discuss with enthusiasm how great we would all look if the socialite could harness their energy and passion when running a project or a task.

Finally, I also noticed other changes happening within my own mental state and motivation. I was still a competitive and direct person, but I also became more considerate and caring, more fun and charismatic (and better at presenting) and more accurate and systematic in how I ran my company and took decisions. In short, I started to gain some of the positive attributes from each of the other styles.

In summary, I could say that I learned a very valuable lesson.

You should not speak to people in the way in which you would like to be spoken to, as this actually shows very little respect or understanding. It can lead to miscommunication, dislike, lack of engagement and, ultimately, conflict.

You should speak to people in the way in which they would like to be spoken to. This shows a very high level of respect and understanding and ensures that your message is far more likely to be understood and acted upon.

You may choose to do this for one or all of the following reasons:

- It is a kind and ethical thing to do (friend reason).
- It will mean that people like and admire you even more (socialite reason).
- It will lead to better results and greater success (challenger reason).
- It is the intelligent thing to do (expert reason).

Exercise

How to use this tool in your own situation

It is remarkably easy to use the CRT styles system to improve your own communication skills. Simply follow these steps:

1. Identify your own preferred styles. Probably you have a good idea of this already, just from reading the descriptions in this book.

2. However, if you need a little more help in identifying your style, try explaining the system to people who know you well and ask them what they think. Do not be surprised if you get different answers from work colleagues and family members, by the way.

It is quite possible to be more friend at home and challenger at work, or more socialite at home and expert at work. Generally, you will find that the home you is the real you and the work you is what you feel you need to become to do your job.

 You can also do the online questionnaire at: www.thebusinessgym.net

3. Identify the styles of the stakeholders and individuals of the team that you need to communicate with. If you are unsure, check with others.

 You can even get other people to have a go at the reflective questionnaire at: www.thebusinessgym.net

4. Decide how you will approach them, i.e. what you will tone down in your own communication style and what you will start doing more of in order to be able to relate to them better.

Use the table below to help create your three-step communication plan.

I am: (add your own communication and motivation preference here)		
Names of people I need to communicate with: (e.g. staff, stakeholders, own line manager)	**I perceive their CRT style as:**	**To communicate well I need to:** (detail what is important to this style so you know to focus on it in your conversation; also note how fast you should talk and the kind of words you should use)

I am: (*Continued*)		
Names of people I need to communicate with:	I perceive their CRT style as:	To communicate well I need to:

Call to action

Answer the following questions honestly. If you are working with a learning group, then share the answers.

- With whom do you need to adapt your communication style?
- What challenges might you face when doing this?
- How can you overcome that?
- What might happen if you do not adapt your communication style with this person or people?
- What will be the benefit or reward if you are able to adapt your communication style?
- How much time will you save over the next year by having more effective conversations, less conflict, more engaged teams and a better relationship with your own line manager?

In one sentence

You should not speak to people in the way in which you would like to be spoken to; you should speak to people in the way in which they would like to be spoken to.

 You can view a podcast that summarises the main points of this step at:

www.thebusinessgym.net

Step 3

How to build trust

After reading this step you will:

- Understand the basic components of trust
- Be able to analyse how likely people are to trust you to lead them
- Be able to take action to build increased trust with your staff, line manager, stakeholders and clients.

Case study

Part 1: Example situation

'*A simple truth about leadership people: there are times in leadership when the trust of your team, peers or manager is the greatest commodity you can have .'*

Here are three situations where trust or, in some cases, a lack of it, has had a profound impact on a project or an organisation:

1. A senior leader instigating change throughout their organisation. They have known that the change will benefit everyone greatly, including their own staff. However, because their teams have not trusted them enough (they have not believed what the leader was saying), overcoming the resistance to change has become back-breaking work.

2. A leader running critical projects, where knowing what was working well and where possible problems lay, would mean the difference between great success and catastrophic failure. Because the project staff did not feel they could safely mention where mistakes were happening without being hung out to dry or angrily blamed, they did what any sensible person would do in that situation – they kept quiet. This is another example where the leader, having the trust of their staff, could have saved the day. A skilled leadership speaker called Patrick Lencioni calls this vulnerability-based trust. If people feel vulnerable (at risk) when they are communicating something bad, then they are very unlikely to communicate it.

3. Finally, here is a positive example of what trust can achieve. This is where a few under-resourced individuals have gone to extreme lengths to achieve what others had described as impossible. They did this because they trusted their leader, believed their leader and had faith in their leader's vision.

Trust is important. For a leader, lack of trust will always lead to long-term failure. In this step we will explore the three basic components that make up trust. We will also detail how you can build it and keep it.

As your trainer/coach, if I have done my job well, then by the time you get to the end of this step you should realise how easy it is to build trust with your team. Also, you will have an effective plan for doing this.

Self-reflection

- How willing are your staff to speak openly and honestly to you about problems or mistakes? Do they come to you as soon as they make or spot a mistake so that something can be done to remedy it? Do they ever hide things from you or try to cover mistakes up?
- How willing are your team to embrace changes that you make?
- How much do you think your team trust you?
- How much do you think your manager or stakeholders trust you?
- How much do you think this affects the success of your team and, therefore, your career?
- What could you achieve if your team trusted you completely?
- What could you achieve if your manager and stakeholders trusted you completely?

Tool or model

A few years ago, a friend, colleague and leadership coach called Phil Holder introduced me to a formula for trust that he devised in 2003. He called it the trust equation. We had some interesting discussions around this. If you run an internet search on the term trust equation, you will get hundreds of different equations and I am sorry to report that, generally, they are baloney and very easy to disprove. So, at first, I was quite biased and felt that anything named the trust equation would not hold much interest for me.

Whilst I disagreed with the exact details of Phil's original equation, I found that the components he named were deeply insightful and very useful to reflect upon. I changed the model slightly and presented it to senior leaders to fit with my own experience, showing how it could give great insight into how trust is created and lost. It could also help leaders to analyse if their team trusted them enough, for them to successfully ask the team to take on a task that was either very risky or very difficult. I have taught my version of the trust equation for a couple of years now and delegate feedback has been that it is an important part of understanding what makes good leadership.

First, we will look at the adapted equation, then we will explore its component parts and discover how we can use our knowledge of this to build the trust of your teams, stakeholders and line managers.

 Trust = (perceived credibility + perceived empathy) − perceived risk

Perceived credibility

The first thing to notice here is the word perceived. It is an important word because trust is not about what is going on your head, it is about what is going on in the other person's head. For example, you may think you are utterly reliable but, if the person does not think you are reliable, they are not going to trust you. Trust is not about what you think of yourself, it is about what other people think about you. Trust is to do with their perception of you, not your perception of yourself. This is the same if we look at it from a different angle, i.e. what affects how much you trust someone else?

One thing is how credible you think they are. They may think that they are utterly credible but, if you do not agree (if your perception is that they are not credible), then you will not trust them.

Our perception of someone's credibility is based upon two things:

1. What we have experienced **directly,** for example, how often have they been right, do they always stick to their word and do they do what they say they are going to do?

2. What we experience **indirectly** or through inference, for example, what do others say about them, what do their qualifications imply or infer about them, what do their colleagues or the company they keep imply about them?

Here are some examples to demonstrate these points.

Direct experience

- You attend your doctor's surgery for a minor complaint. Your doctor has always helped you in the past and always seemed to be spot on in her diagnoses. How credible would you describe your doctor as being?

- You attend your doctor's surgery for a minor complaint. Your doctor has always tried to help you in the past but clearly has been wrong in a couple of his initial diagnoses in the past. This meant that you took unnecessary medication for a short while. How credible would you describe your doctor as being?

- You are on holiday in another country and visit a doctor's surgery because of a minor complaint. You have no previous experience with this doctor and do not know if the country's doctors are famous for being good, bad or average. How credible would you describe the doctor as being?

Indirect or inferred experience

- You have a minor complaint but choose to visit a specialist. Before walking into the doctor's consulting room, you notice that there are a number of qualifications and accreditations hanging on the wall that show that the doctor is a specialist in his field. You have also noticed that the doctor has a lot of letters after his name (far more than your regular GP has). How credible would you describe the doctor as being?

- You have a minor complaint but choose to visit a specialist. Before attending, you do an internet search and find a number of people have complained that the specialist misdiagnosed them, which meant that they underwent procedures that they did not need. How credible would you describe the doctor as being?

- You have a minor complaint but choose to visit a specialist. When you walk into the consulting room, you realise that you recognise the doctor as being part of a group of drunken trouble makers in a restaurant you visited last night. You did not notice the doctor herself making trouble, but the people she was clearly friends with caused a scene, threw up due to the amount of alcohol they had drunk and, generally, made everyone else in the restaurant feel uncomfortable. How credible would you describe the doctor as being?

The things we do, as well as what people say about us, our qualifications, job title and the company we keep, all affect how credible we are perceived to be.

Always remember: your reputation is important! Luckily, you are the person who has the biggest impact on it. It is up to you whether you stick to your word, are honest about what you do and do not know, treat people well, can be relied upon and are willing to do the right thing (all hallmarks of a good manager/leader who can be trusted). It is for this reason that I believe in what I call reality karma. Personally, I do not believe in a mystical Buddhist energy that permeates the universe. But I do believe that what we put out into the world and how we interact with others does come back to affect us.

(Additional note: if you do believe in the Buddhist version of karma, then great – I fully support you in your beliefs. If everyone in the world shared your personal views of karma, then I suspect that the world would be a better place to live in for all of us!)

Perceived empathy

Perceived empathy is an interesting thing to discuss and, again, the key word here is perceived. Empathy is our ability to understand someone else's emotions, situation and point of view. If we believe (or perceive) someone has empathy with us, we think that they get us or can understand where we are coming from. If someone can empathise with us, then they can relate to us, whether we are frustrated, joyous or fearful. Remember, it is the perception of empathy that is so vital here.

Let us assume you meet a random person on the street. Before you have even spoken to them, how much empathy do you perceive them to have of you and your situation? I suspect the answer is not much. Now, what if I tell you that they are a telepath? As soon as they saw you, they could hear your thoughts, sense your emotions – your fears, needs, desires and concerns – and know everything that has happened to you. Undoubtedly, they would be able to have great empathy with you. But, until you found out they were a telepath, you would still perceive them as having little or no empathy with you. A good leader who wants the trust of their team needs not only to have empathy, but also to actively show that they have it!

(I should make it clear here that I am not suggesting that there are actual telepaths wandering the streets of your local town or city; this is just a thought exercise to demonstrate a point.)

Luckily, there is a very easy way to build and show empathy. It takes a little time, but is not difficult and can be done by anyone – you simply ask questions.

To understand and, therefore, empathise with people, we need to find out about them. To show that we understand them, we simply need to show that we are asking questions and listening to the answers. To build empathy, try asking someone what their hopes, fears, thoughts and feelings are and show that you are listening to their answers. By the way, one of the quickest ways to show a lack of empathy is to ask these questions and then completely ignore the answers.

When training, before I ask my leadership groups to do something that might take them out of their comfort zone, often I will ask them how they are feeling. I will ask if the room temperature is ok for them or if the group needs a quick break or if anyone needs to get a glass of water, etc. I will listen to their answers and act accordingly, for example, turning on the air conditioning or heating, encouraging people to nip to the loo, get a quick coffee or just stretch their legs. These simple questions and actions give the delegates the perception that I have empathy for them. It helps them realise that I care about their comfort and understand how they are feeling. In fact, often I will ask people in my workshops these exact questions just before I give a demonstration of the trust equation, which I will explain in the following perceived risk section.

Perceived credibility and perceived empathy go a long way to building our sense of trust in another human being. They are two important components. If we perceive someone as credible and believe that they get us or understand our feelings and the situation we are in, then we are more likely to trust them. However, they are not the only components of trust, because trust is context sensitive, i.e. trust also depends on the situation we are in.

Perceived risk

Imagine that someone you know and love (perhaps your partner, a very good friend or trusted family member) asks you to close your eyes and hold out your hands, palms up, because they want to give you a present – would you do it?

The chances are that you would. Perhaps you might be a little suspicious, especially if the person you know and love has played harmless practical jokes on you in the past (direct experience affecting your perception of their credibility). However, generally, most of us would agree because there is a very low risk of something bad happening and a good chance that we will get something nice. Plus we might just be curious.

Now imagine that a stranger on the street, who you have never met before, asked you exactly the same thing. Would you still do it?

The chances are that you would not and it is not just because of perceived credibility and perceived empathy. Now perceived risk is playing an important role! Why have they asked me to do this? Even if they promise a present, we might suspect that there is, actually, a risk that they will run off with our wallets whilst we stand with our eyes closed and hands outstretched.

In my leadership training sessions, often I use a variant of this exercise. First, very deliberately, I peel an orange or satsuma in front of everyone. Also, I comment that, although oranges are good for you and taste nice, they can be very sticky. (Anyone who has spent time with a young child knows just how sticky an orange can be!) Next I ask all my delegates to stand up, hold their right hand open, palm up, and then to close their eyes until I give them further instructions. Then I walk around the room, making heavy footfalls so that each person knows when I am standing in front of them. I am pleased to say that, as yet, every single delegate has done as I have asked and not opened their eyes until instructed to do so. I believe it is because, by this time in the course, I have built enough credibility and empathy with them that it outweighs the very small perceived risk that I might put a sticky piece of orange in their hands. Then I ask them to open their eyes, sit down and relax, and ask them, 'What was the perceived risk?' Some people say there was not one. Most respond and confess that they were a little worried in case I put a sticky piece of fruit in their hands. In each case, the perceived risk is very small and their perception of my credibility and empathy for them easily outweighs the risk. It should be noted that, as I mentioned earlier, normally, very deliberately, I will ask them how they are feeling just before I start this exercise. This provides me with a boost in their perception of my empathy for them.

Next I ask, hypothetically, 'If I asked you all to come to the roof of this building with me, where I will tie a piece of rope around you, which I will hold on to, and ask you to lean out over the edge of the building until you are parallel with the road five floors below, who would be willing to trust me and have a go?' From a room of 12 people, all of whom were completely ok to trust me when the perceived risk was small (something sticky placed in the hand), very few people are willing to trust me enough to let me hypothetically dangle them from the roof of a five-storey building. In this situation, their perception of my credibility or empathy for them has not changed; what has changed is the level of risk that they perceive.

(Occasionally, I will have some daring soul who says yes, they would trust me to do this. In these situations, I thank them for their faith in me and then ask them how they would feel if I did the experiment with their children, pets or partners. Aside from some typically very funny answers relating to how much stress children, pets and partners can cause us, the general consensus is that it would make people feel very uncomfortable indeed!)

Case study

Part 2: How the example situation was resolved

As a leader, we should always be aware of how much trust our people have in us. We should also be aware of how this can change, depending on the situation and the perceived risk.

 When managing change, it is vital to be honest (build perceived credibility), listen to people's fears and concerns (build perceived empathy) and discuss the risks realistically and openly instead of allowing people's imaginations to run wild (minimise the perceived level of risk).

When managing change projects, classic errors include:

- telling everyone it will be painless when clearly it will not be (damages credibility and perceived empathy)
- not listening to people's fears and simply demanding that they need to be positive and to trust that the senior leadership team knows best (again, damages perceived credibility, empathy and actually raises the perception of risk instead of lowering it)
- having long drawn-out consultation periods, without clearly identifying who may be at risk and who is definitely not at risk (raises perceived level of risk and harms perception of empathy).

By avoiding these common mistakes and being aware of the trust equation, it is quite possible to instigate major change programmes with minimal resistance.

In any team it is vital that members of staff feel free to raise their fears and concerns without fear of blame or retribution. Where leaders show that they will listen to staff and understand that mistakes can happen (be credible and have empathy), and that they are approachable and will not shoot the messenger (low perceived risk), then staff will openly alert project leaders to major problems, thus possibly saving the project or task from critical failure.

Ultimately, leaders who are aware of the trust equation and actively build a high level of trust with their teams will find that these teams will go the extra mile for them and may surprise everyone with their level of conviction, engagement, dedication and loyalty.

 **Exercise**

How to use this tool in your own situation

To use the trust equation in your own situation you will need to simply focus on the three components:

1. What is your level of credibility with the team, your line manager or stakeholders at the moment? What can you do to enhance that? Remember that being honest, doing what you

say you are going to do and sticking to your word are all vital. But it is not just direct experience that affects credibility. What are other people in the business or industry saying about you? How should you choose to act in the future in order to ensure your reputation goes from strength to strength?

2. How much do people perceive that you empathise with them? Ask questions and find out about what people are thinking, feeling, hoping and fearing. You do not need to interview or 'grill' them. Just start having some honest conversations with them when you ask them questions and then you shut up and listen to the answers. Show you are listening. Adapting your communication style using the combined reflective tool (CRT) is a great thing to do here.

3. If you need someone to trust you, consider what risks they may be perceiving or, even better, ask and find out what risk they perceive. Work to minimise the level of threat posed by those risks (in their perception), thereby allowing greater trust.

Call to action

Answer the following questions honestly. If you are working with a learning group, then share the answers.

- How confident are you at the moment that your team trust you?

  (No one likes to admit that they are not trusted but, if you have answered 'very confident', on what evidence are you basing your perception?)

- How confident are you at the moment that your line manager and stakeholders trust you?

  (What evidence are you basing your perception on?)

- Using the trust equation, what can you start doing to increase their trust in you (even if their level of trust is already high)?

- What might hinder you as you try to do this?

- How can you overcome that?

- What might happen if your team, manager or stakeholders do not completely trust you?

- What will be the benefit or reward to you if they do?

In one sentence

When people decide whether to trust you or not, their decision is based on three things: how credible they think you are, how much they think you empathise with their situation and how much risk there is in what you are asking them to do.

 You can view a podcast that summarises the main points of this step at:

www.thebusinessgym.net

Step 4

Adapting your leadership style for the best outcome

After reading this step you will:

- Be able to analyse your staff members' levels of competence and confidence

- Understand how to adapt your style of leadership for each individual you manage (based on their competence and confidence)

- Understand why the two points above are so important to successful leadership.

Case study

Part 1: Example situation

- You have asked someone to do something. You have shown them very clearly exactly what to do and offered lots of support as they do it, but they seem to be really disengaged and keep making silly mistakes. Instead of seeing you as supportive, they think you are a micromanager or control freak.

- You have asked someone to do something that, according to their job role, they should definitely be able to do. Because they should know what they are doing, you have left them to get on with it but later found they have either made lots of mistakes or have avoided doing the task altogether. Instead of basking in their independence and the trust you have shown them, they feel that they are lost, have been set up to fail, or that you are placing unreasonable demands on them.

We have identified the traits of a good leader and bad leader, but the good leader was flexible in their leadership style. Sometimes, they gave lots of direction and support, sometimes they simply trusted staff to get on with the job. Traditionally, these two sides of leadership are referred to as an autocratic style and a laissez-faire style (see the following figure).

One of the skills you need as a good manager is the ability to be adaptable and flexible with your management style. As in any training regime, flexibility is a key strength and it is important to practise it. Commonly, there are three main times when a lack of awareness of the need to be flexible with leadership style can cause a problem:

1. When a manager is using an autocratic style but has team members that feel they are just being micromanaged and treated with little respect for skills or knowledge. This is common when the manager simply has been used to managing new and inexperienced staff or when it is how the manager themself has been managed.

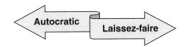

Autocratic style involves giving clear direction, specific instruction and keeping control.
With an autocratic style of management, staff have little or no freedom to make mistakes. When done at the right time, an autocratic style is perceived as being a strong management style. When done at the wrong time, it is perceived as micromanaging.

Laissez-faire is a French term that literally means allow to do. The *Oxford English Dictionary* defines it as 'The policy of leaving things to take their own course, without interfering'. This style focuses on trusting staff to use their own knowledge and skills to do something the correct way. Staff receive a very hands-off style of management and have maximum freedom to implement plans as they see fit. When done at the right time, this is perceived as liberating and engaging. When done at the wrong time, it leaves staff feeling directionless, unsupported, confused, doubtful and lacking in confidence.

Autocratic and laissez-faire styles

2. When a manager is using a laissez-faire style because they want to encourage staff and show that they are trusted. However, staff are in desperate need of clearer direction, support and control. This is common when the manager likes and respects the team members but does not realise that they lack confidence, skill or knowledge (i.e. experience) in what they are doing.

3. When someone has been promoted or given new tasks because they were great at their old role, and are managed with a laissez-faire style. What they actually need is clear direction and instruction because, whilst they were experienced in their old role, they are inexperienced in their new post.

Self-reflection

- Are you able to adapt your management style to different people in different situations? If so, how do you decide whether to be autocratic, laissez-faire or somewhere in between?

- Are you confident that you are getting the best out of your staff? Are your experienced people still engaged and motivated? Are your less experienced people comfortable with asking lots of questions whilst they become acquainted with the role?

- Do you ever feel that your own managers and peers expect you to know things in your new role that actually you are struggling with? (If you do, do not worry. It is very common and this next tool will not only help you understand why it happens, but also how to fix the problem.)

 You may like to test your natural leadership style by taking the leadership questionnaire online at:

www.thebusinessgym.net

Tool or model

Progressive leadership model (PLM)

With this model we will be using the word competence a lot. Competence basically means the ability to do the job. Competence is a combination of knowledge, skill, motivation and confidence.

Whilst competence often comes with experience, it is important to remember that that the two are not inexorably linked. It is quite possible for someone with a limited amount of experience to be competent; they may be naturally gifted in the subject area or perfectly suited to the role. Equally, an individual may have many years of experience but still be viewed as incompetent by others; this may be because of a lack of knowledge, skill, motivation or confidence.

The idea of progressive leadership simply states that,

> 'as the competence of your staff progresses, your management and leadership style should also progress'.

That is, a good manager or leader is one who adapts and flexes their leadership style, depending on the person's competence with the task at hand.

I created the progressive leadership model to illustrate how we can chart a team member's progress and then choose the

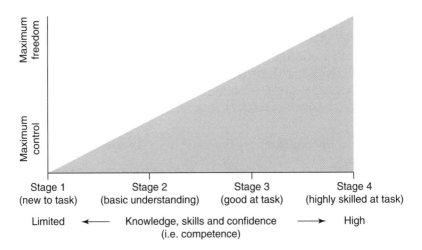

The progressive leadership model – as the knowledge, skill and confidence of a staff member progresses, so should our leadership style

correct leadership approach for them (see the following figure). However, I did not come up with the original idea. As long as there have been chains of leadership in governments and armies, good leaders have known to give greater freedom and trust to people who show competence. The idea can be traced back to the ancient Greeks and Romans and I am sure worthy historians would find that the idea has deeper roots than even those.

Throughout the modern world, most military forces now work the principles of progressive leadership and increased autonomy based on ability (competence). First, soldiers are drilled repeatedly and given strict discipline and instruction in order to gain a high level of competence in basic manoeuvres or combat procedures. As the soldier gains experience, confidence, knowledge and skills, they are expected to show a higher level of autonomy, self-reliance and decision-making ability. This, ultimately, leads to highly competent squads who are given objectives by their military commanders, and then make their own decisions on the best way to achieve these objectives – based on the situation and context in which they find themselves.

In fact, battles, and even wars, have been won by the side that has had military units able to show a greater level of initiative, autonomy and the ability to adapt to new circumstances and situations. Many of the world's elite forces, such as the SAS, Navy SEALs, GSG 9 and GSGN, are staffed by extremely competent individuals, used to working in a very autonomous way.

Staff progress	Description	Typical situation	Leadership style
Stage 1	New to task, role or project	First day, initial training	**Autocratic style – high tell/low ask** Maximum control, explicit instructions with examples and monitoring
Stage 2	Good basic understanding of task, role or project	Some experience in role or task	**Discussive style – high tell/high ask** Instruction, with some freedom, high control, high level of support but with some freedom for exploration
Stage 3	High level of understanding of task, role or project	Considered experienced and capable at task	**Coaching style – low tell/high ask** High freedom, some instruction, challenge and coach to expert level
Stage 4	Highly skilled at task, role or project	Considered expert in task, e.g. subject matter expert (SME)	**Partnering style – no tell/high ask** Complete freedom to achieve agreed objectives how they see fit (very low control), challenge and delegate new task areas and responsibilities

As a team member's competence progresses, so should the leader's style of management and leadership; initially managed with maximum control and detailed instruction, eventually managed with minimum control (high freedom) and low instruction.

In stage 1, an autocratic style works best. This can be thought of as high tell/low ask, i.e. you do lots of telling/instructing. When a member of staff is new to the job, it is likely that their competence with the new role will be limited (their motivation may be high, but their knowledge, skill and confidence are likely to be low). In these situations, an individual will need clear instruction and close monitoring. They need lots of direction, guidance and hands-on management until they grow in competence.

In stage 2, a discussive style works best. As the member of staff becomes more experienced in the role and, hopefully, more competent (knowledge, skills and confidence start to increase), you may start to be a little less controlling and directive in your management style. This can be thought of as high tell/high ask. At this stage, you still want to instruct the individual (high tell), but you also want to start discussing the situations with them to help grow their understanding and skills (high ask). It is important to invite comments and lots of questions at this stage.

In stage 3, a coaching style works best. Now the team member is skilled and reasonably confident in the role, your aim is to show them how to solve problems and find solutions by themselves. Try to shift to asking not telling (low tell/high ask) when interacting with individuals at this stage. You may still need to give answers occasionally but you also want to start giving them the freedom to explore systems on their own and possibly even make mistakes (sometimes the mistakes you make will teach you more than your successes). Try setting an objective and asking the team member how they will achieve it, instead of telling them how they will achieve it.

In stage 4, a partnership style works best. (Sometimes known as a consultative style.) If a member of staff is highly competent in a role, show them that you trust their skill and judgement and let them get on with it. Micromanaging staff who are highly competent is a sure fire way of demotivating them and is likely to lead to a decrease in confidence (as they wonder why you do not trust them) and, therefore, a decrease in competence (as they start to second guess themselves).

In this stage, a good leader will adopt a no tell/high ask approach. They may act towards the team member as if they were a partner, discussing objectives and timescales with the team member and allowing them the freedom to proceed as they see fit.

At this stage, the team member may often be considered the subject matter expert (SME), in which case they are likely to understand the particular details of their field of specialisation better than the manager does. This is a positive situation and nothing to be afraid of, as it means that the manager can now consult with the team member.

Developing your team to the point where they are all highly competent in their fields, and able to truly advise you as to the best way that they can contribute towards your overall team goal, is a wonderful thing. It will lead to success! Only a weak manager feels the need to always know more than all of their team members, as this can be achieved in only two ways.

1. Spend all your time swotting up in the areas where you employ people to do the job for you (and therefore do not spend your time getting on with your own job or actually managing the team).

2. Keep your team deliberately ignorant (a plan that clearly has so many problems connected with it, it hardly seems worth discussing here).

 It is perfectly ok to have team members in different stages. Part of good succession planning is recognising that people will progress and, as the leader, you should encourage this. This also means you will need new people coming through in stage 1 and learning skills from the people in stage 4.

You can be in stage 1 any time you are experiencing something new or learning new skills. If a high-performing individual (in stage 4) is promoted or given a new type of challenge, they are likely to move to stage 1 in relation to their new role or challenge.

It is, therefore, possible for an individual to be in two places on the model at once. For example, stage 4 for their core job role or function and stage 1 for a new project or task.

On this basis, the progressive leadership model actually should be an upwards spiral, with skilled employees regularly passing through all stages as they learn new skills, adapt to new challenges and are promoted (see the following figure).

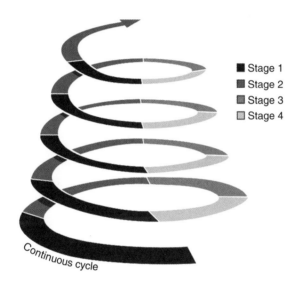

Stage 1
Stage 2
Stage 3
Stage 4

Continuous cycle

It is important that stage 4 staff understand that a new task or role may place them in stage 1 and that it is perfectly ok for them to ask questions. An example of this is when a highly skilled member of staff is promoted to become a supervisor or leader.

Case study

Part 2: How the example situation was resolved

1. Using the wrong style with an individual can lead to disengagement and mistakes. A leader who is more used to using an autocratic style can plot their team members on the chart and see how they need to change their management style for different individuals.

2. This is equally true for leaders who naturally prefer using a laissez-faire style. By choosing the right level of progressive leadership style for any individual, we can help their development, motivation and confidence. By choosing the wrong style, we will actively harm or damage their development, motivation and confidence.

Remember, whenever someone is promoted or given a new task or responsibility, they may be moving into a stage 1 situation. Even if they are firmly in stage 4 for their old role or core responsibilities, the leader should ensure that the individual receives relevant training and support for their new situation.

There are two valuable ways for you to use the progressive leadership model:

1. When considering how to develop and lead your staff.

2. When you are considering your own career development and job satisfaction.

 **Exercise**

How to use this tool in your own situation

1. When considering your own staff

Plot where each member of staff is on the progressive leadership scale. The further up and to the right they are, i.e. the more skill, knowledge and confidence they have, the more you need to allow them freedom (laissez-faire style). The closer to the bottom left they are, i.e. less skill, knowledge and confidence, the more they will need clear instruction, monitoring and control (autocratic style).

Look at the progressive leadership model (on **page 53**) again. As the knowledge, skill and confidence of a staff member progresses, so should our leadership style.

Practise adapting and flexing your leadership style to get the best out of different members of your team in different situations.

Remember, it is quite possible for someone in your team to be in two or more places at once on the progressive leadership scale. Do not be surprised if you start to have conversations that go something like this:

Stage 4 Partnership style	'Yasmina, I have an objective that I would like you to look at, please. As the expert in this field, I need you to review what we are trying to achieve and then create a project plan for the best way to move forward on this, plus your general recommendations.'
Stages 2 and 3 Discussive and coaching styles used together	'When you have worked out a plan you are happy with, we will need to sit down together and create a resourcing proposal for the board. I will show you the templates we use and then we can feed your figures in.'
Stage 1 leading to stage 2 Autocratic leading to discussive style	'Your work on these kinds of projects is excellent, so, once the project goes live, I think it would be good for you to run the budget forecasting as well. It is a good skill to learn, as it will help you see more of what is happening in the company at a higher level and why. I know this is new you to you, so I will book you on some training and also support you as you create your first few financial forecasts. How does this sound to you?,

The progressive leadership model also makes a great tool for performance improvement and development conversations. By having an open, two-way conversation with staff about where they are on the progressive scale, staff can see quickly where they need to improve and where they might want to start taking on new challenges:

'Karen, let's break down your role into its five core areas or disciplines: project planning, stakeholder management, financial control, reporting and risk.

'Where would you place yourself on the progressive leadership scale with regards to your knowledge, skills, motivation and confidence in each area? So, what are the next steps for developing in each area?'

2. When you feel that you have less knowledge than others expect you to have, or that you know your own job so well you desperately need a new challenge

Recognise where you are on the progressive leadership scale. If you are at stage 1 or 2 because you have just been promoted or taken on a new type of task, do not be afraid to ask for more help! Getting extra instruction and support will mean you will be able to quickly master your new role or task, instead of floundering, failing and being thought of as incompetent. If you are at stage 3 or 4, then start thinking proactively about where else you might want to develop. Go to your own line manager or director with a range of new tasks that you would like to take on.

With regards to asking for help

Often, new leaders worry that they will look weak or stupid if they ask for more direction or training. If you share this concern, then try answering these three simple questions:

1 Would you rather one of your staff said that they did not know how to do something, or carried on pretending that they did, whilst hoping to hell that they were able to pick it up before anyone important noticed?

2 What would be the impact of the two options mentioned above?

3 Who would you respect the most: the person who asks for instruction and then does their job well, or the person who hides their incompetence and gets found out only when a critical mistake is made?

Looking at the progressive leadership model (**page 53**) again, plot each member of your team on the scale to see which style of leadership is best. Then plot where *you* are to check where you need to develop, or seek out new challenges.

Call to action

Answer the following questions honestly. If you are working with a learning group, then share the answers.

- With whom do you think you might need to adapt your leadership style?
- What might stop you doing this?
- How can you overcome that?
- What might happen if you do not adapt your leadership style with this person?
- What will happen to the levels of engagement and development with members of your team, if you adapt your leadership style to suit their needs?
- How will understanding your own development needs help you as a manager?

In one sentence

Your leadership style should not depend on your preference; it should depend on how your staff need you to lead them.

 You can view a podcast that summarises the main points of this step at:

www.thebusinessgym.net

Step 5

Setting objectives that work

After reading this step you will:

- Be aware of the most common mistakes made when setting objectives

- Understand how these mistakes can be avoided and, in doing so, ensure that the objectives you set are more likely to be met

- Be in a better position to ensure that you can meet the objectives that you are set.

Case study

Part 1: Example situation

The following is a real situation from a global bank that I have worked with in the UK. It shows a typical problem that arises when objectives are not communicated properly. (Names and titles have been changed, expletives have been edited and softened.)

Frank ran a team of data analysts. In addition to their core role, they also undertook some database administration duties for the main database from which they drew their figures.

One day, Frank's manager and head of division, Sam, approached him in a foul mood.

'Frank, I am receiving complaints about the database again from another head of division,' Sam barked. 'This is your team's responsibility and you need to bloody well sort it out! I want you to make sure the database is accurate so that Martin stops complaining and bringing it up in our meetings. Get it done!' Martin was the other head of division and the meetings that Sam was referring to were the Monday morning senior managers' meetings with the operational director.

Frank spent the next two weeks with his team, diligently checking the accuracy of the data in the database. Other work was put on hold temporarily and started to back up as this high priority issue was dealt with. Frank's team also stayed late a number of times to ensure that the task was done as quickly and effectively as possible, with the minimum impact on normal operations.

After two weeks, Frank proudly reported back to Sam that his team had worked hard over the last two weeks to ensure data accuracy and had corrected the few errors that had been found. Sam got even angrier than he had been two weeks ago. Sam had received yet another complaint from Martin that very morning, so he knew Frank's team had not fixed the problem he wanted fixed. Frustrated, he started shouting at Frank, 'You mean you have just spent two weeks and five people's time fixing something that should have taken one person no more than 15 minutes! And you haven't even flipping done it!' Frank walked away, confused, berated and demotivated. Frank's team had witnessed all of this and were also deeply demotivated by what had happened.

Whilst there are a number of issues we could discuss here, including Sam's ability to give constructive feedback and his use of offensive language (Sam used a much more aggressive word than flipping), the issue we are going to explore is the obvious breakdown in communication of the task and objectives.

Self-reflection

As a manager or a leader you will be set objectives yourself and you will, in turn, set objectives for your team. Think of when your team, or a member of your team, has focused on the wrong part of the objective. Why do you suspect this happened?

Perhaps your member of staff was focused on the wrong thing, perhaps they did not actually have the skills or understanding to do the task. Or maybe it just turned out that there were not enough resources (time or money) to do something that initially you thought was achievable.

As a leader, it is vital that, if you set an objective or delegate a task, you know that it will be carried out and completed correctly.

 **Exercise**

Either by yourself, or in your learning group, complete the table below.

When I am set an objective, if I am to succeed then it is important that:	I find it difficult to meet an objective if it is delegated in the following way:

Tool or model

Here are the five golden rules for setting objectives. They are listed in order of how frequently they are missed and their importance.

1. Objective setting should be a **two-way conversation**. Objective setting and delegation should be a discussion, not just an instruction.

2. Both sides should understand exactly **what** needs to be done and how success will be measured. This understanding should always be checked via a two-way conversation (see rule 1 above).

3. Both sides should understand **why** something needs to be done, the impact it will have if accomplished and the impact it will have if not accomplished. Here the actual or real goal is normally identified. **Why** something needs to be done is an integral part of explaining **what** needs to be done.

4. Both sides should agree, genuinely, that the task is **achievable,** based realistically on resources available. It is often easy to get someone to agree that a task is achievable, when in reality it is not. Workloads, priorities and resources should all be reality-checked. Again, the best way to do this is with an open, two-way conversation.

5. The person or team doing the task should understand why they, in particular, are doing it, i.e. **w**hat's **in it** for **t**hem (known as a **WIIFT**). Where possible, tasks should grow or develop the people doing them. Whilst this is not always possible, tasks should at least be spread fairly across teams and departments and appropriate recognition should be given for completed tasks or projects.

Now let us explore them in more detail.

1. Objective setting should be a two-way conversation

The biggest single reason that people fail to deliver an objective is the lack of a two-way conversation. When setting objectives and delegating tasks, be sure to talk **with** people **not at** them. Allow the person to whom you are delegating to repeat back their understanding of what needs to be done, why it needs to be done, and by when it needs to be done. Ask them how they will fit it in to their existing workload and, if the answer is, 'I will find a way,' ask them specifically what they will do. Be warned that, 'I will find a way' often is code for:

> *'I am really busy right now and I do not actually know when I will find the time to do this. I guess I will just have to try and squeeze it in and either it will not get done in time or to the quality you want, or something else will fail or not get done on time because of this.'*

2. and 3. Be specific about what needs to get done, by when, and why it needs to be done

The clearest way to do this to discuss how success will be measured, i.e. by what criteria you will deem the task a success.

 Exercise

Consider how you would react and what you would focus on if you were set these three simple tasks:

1. Design or source a simple box that can carry 1,000 A4 pieces of paper. 100 boxes will be needed. The task will be deemed a success if the design is complete within the next five minutes. The boxes will be needed the day after tomorrow in order to relocate our office paperwork to the new office next door.

   • What would you focus on here?

   Most groups I give this exercise to sketch a simple cardboard box because it is quick, simple and readily available.

2. Design or source a simple box that can carry 1,000 A4 pieces of paper. 100 boxes will be needed. The task will be deemed a success if the boxes are of sufficient quality to protect the paper from long-term damage, given that the paper will be stored in an old warehouse with a leaky roof. The paper is being stored because of an office move, which is happening in three weeks' time and is likely to take up to six months to complete.

   • What would you focus on here?

Most groups I give this exercise to sketch a plastic box or Tupperware container that could be bought from a local store.

3. Design or source a simple box that can carry 1,000 A4 pieces of paper. 100 boxes will be needed. The task will be deemed a success if the boxes look good, as they will be used to transport advertising literature to our clients and they must impress. The shipment of advertising materials will be going out in three months' time.

    - What would you focus on here?

    Groups that I give this exercise to create a wide array of solutions, from crafted wooden boxes wrapped with ribbons, to sleek futuristic looking metal containers with a stylish branded company logo.

Each task involves designing a box to carry 1,000 A4 sheets of paper. However, because how success will be measured is different in each situation, the resulting three boxes are likely to be different in their design.

How could the box designs change if success was measured by cost to manufacture, security, how supportable or easy to repair the boxes were, durability and reusability, speed to manufacture or the ability to make the boxes without a professional manufacturer?

A successful step 2, understanding what needs to be done and by when, involves step 1, a two-way conversation, and step 3, understanding why it needs to be done.

By understanding the real impact of why something needs to be done, we gain greater clarity on specifically what needs to be done and by when it needs to be done. This understanding also allows the person doing the task to react to changing circumstances in a more effective manner. For example:

Consider the third task set above where we needed to design a box that would also impress a client and was needed in three months' time. If you suddenly found out that you had to have the box ready in three days, or that it could cost no more than £2, you could probably still come up with a design that was deemed a success because it looked good and impressed the client.

4. Both sides should agree, genuinely, that the task is achievable, based realistically on resources available

A task can be achievable theoretically without being achievable realistically. Consider this example:

- In order to progress in your career, I suggest you do a master's degree in management. The master's degree will take one year to complete and you will have two years to complete it. Is this achievable – yes or no?

- Now consider that the degree will take at least 20 hours' work per week. Think about your work, family and social commitments. Is it realistically achievable – yes or no?

Always remember to have an open two-way conversation with the individual for whom you are setting the task, discussing whether it is achievable realistically and, if not, what needs to be done to ensure it can be achieved realistically. This may involve discussing how other work should be prioritised or how additional help and resources can be secured.

In addition, trigger points should be discussed and set here. A trigger point is a situation that triggers another action (normally escalation or reporting). For example, 'If X is not completed by Tuesday, then let me know so that I can get you some help to ensure Y still gets done by Friday.' X not being done by Tuesday has now become a trigger point.

5. Make sure the person doing the task knows what's in it for them (WIIFT)

The best way to do this is to ask the individual what they will get out of the task, whilst ensuring that they understand the development opportunity that the task affords them.

Whilst, ideally, any task should be an opportunity to develop, in reality this is not always the case. Interestingly, however, value can be found in almost any task.

 One of the best ways to help people find value (and therefore motivation) in a task is not to tell them why they should do it and what they can get out of it, but to ask them.

I have been challenged on this many times with different leadership groups. The challenge is always the same – that some tasks just have to be done and there is no real value or reward for the person doing them. However, I have found that this next simple hypothetical exercise demonstrates the solution nicely.

 Exercise

Imagine that this morning your office received a call explaining that the cleaners would no longer be coming in. The old contractor went bankrupt so it is not the fault of anyone in your office that you do not currently have a cleaner. It is expected to take a few days to find a new cleaning contractor and have them actually start.

Meanwhile, you have been asked to take a turn cleaning the office lavatory, which, until today, was cleaned every two hours by the contracted cleaning company. This is not a task that you, personally, will need to do regularly from now on. However, in order to be fair, it is a task that everyone must do at least once while a new office cleaning contractor is found and hired.

In the table below write two key benefits of you cleaning the lavatory.

1
2

Most people find it reasonably easy to identify two benefits. Benefits that people have come up in the past have included: I will have a clean lavatory to use; it will show I am not afraid to do some of the mucky/lowlier/less esteemed jobs; it will show I am fair; it will show I am a team player; I can choose the scent (air-freshener); I can set the standard; I know it is done; and, my personal favourite, it would actually be a welcome break from my highly stressful normal job.

By creating the two benefits in the previous table, you assigned value and worth to the task. You showed something that you could get out of doing the task, even though many business people initially would claim that there is no value to them doing a task such as this.

 The best way to help someone identify the value in a task is not tell to them what the value is, it is to ask them what value they might get out of doing the task.

In summary, if you cannot see a value or a benefit in assigning a task to a particular individual, then at least ensure that tasks are assigned fairly across the team. Be open that a particular objective does not offer a development opportunity but also feel free to ask the individual what they might, possibly, gain from doing the task. And, remember, simple recognition of a task well done can be immensely valuable, even for repetitive jobs or low-profile objectives.

Case study

Part 2: How the example situation was resolved

In the real example I gave at the start of this step, a two-way conversation and understanding how success would be measured would have solved Frank's and Sam's problem. In this situation, the other head of division (Martin) was using information from just one field in the database. Martin needed and expected that information to be given in euros. However, the information was currently in pounds sterling. Sam knew this, but Frank did not. Frank took Sam's instruction to clean up the database literally.

If Sam had stayed calm and asked Frank for his thoughts, Frank probably would have asked, 'What exactly is Martin's issue? Is it ok if I go and ask him what he is finding wrong with the database and what will make him happy?' At which point, Frank would have received answers as part of a two-way conversation and understood that all that needed doing was a currency value change in one field (or box) of the database. The task would take one person only 15 minutes at most, it would make Martin happy, stop the complaints and, therefore, keep Sam happy as well!

 **Exercice**

How to use this tool in your own situation

Whenever you set objectives for your own staff, practise following all five of the golden rules for delegation. You should be especially vigilant when setting tasks that are unusual or completely new to a member of staff.

Whenever you are set tasks, ensure you have the same understanding as your manager of rules 2–5. If they are unwilling to have a two-way conversation about this, at least ask if you can check your understanding with them on the following points: what needs to be done, by when, why, and how success will be measured, what resources will be needed, whether these resources are available, and why you, in particular, have been chosen to do it. This should lead to a positive two-way conversation, even if they were such a poor manager that they did not want one.

Here is a summary of the five golden rules for setting objectives:

1. Have a two-way conversation covering steps 2–5.

2. What needs to be done, by when and how will success be measured?

3. Why does it need to be done, what is the ultimate goal here and, once again, how will success be measured?

4. Is it realistically achievable? If not, what do you need to do to make it achievable? What are the trigger points if things start to go wrong?

5. Why have you asked this person to do the task? What is in it for them, how will it develop them, what recognition or reward will they receive for a job well done?

 Practice

- Think of a task or objective that you have just set for one of your staff. Apply the five golden rules to this scenario. Write a plan of how the conversation could have gone if the five rules were used as a template or checklist.

1. Have a two-way conversation.
2. What needs to be done, by when and how will success be measured?
3. Why does it need to be done? What is the ultimate goal here? Check once again how success will be measured.
4. Is it realistically achievable? If not, what do you need to do to make it achievable? What are the trigger points if things start to go wrong?
5. Why have you asked this person to do the task? What is in it for them, how will it develop them, what recognition or reward will they receive for a job well done?

- Think of a task or objective that you need to set one of your staff in the near future. Apply the five golden rules to this scenario. Again, write a plan of how the conversation should go, using the five golden rules as a template or checklist.
- Think of a task that you have recently been set. Were the five golden rules followed? If not, what do you need to check or know in order to ensure you are successful with the task?

Call to action

Answer the following questions honestly. If you are working with a learning group, then share the answers.

- How will using the five golden rules as a template or checklist help you:
  o with your staff?
  o with your own manager?
- What will be the benefit or reward for you in both situations?
- What might stop you applying the five rules?
- How can you overcome these challenges?
- How much time will you save over the next year by having more effective conversations, less conflict, more engaged teams and a better relationship with your own line manager?

In one sentence

Only by understanding why something needs doing, can we truly understand how success will be measured.

 You can view a podcast that summarises the main points of this step at:

www.thebusinessgym.net

Step **6**

Delegating to and up-skilling your team

After reading this step you will:

- Be aware of what prevents you delegating
- Understand the implications of not successfully delegating
- Have a framework for deciding what tasks to delegate and to whom to delegate them
- Be able to delegate even mundane and repetitive tasks in an engaging manner.

The manager's dilemma, 'But it is quicker if I do it myself.'

Case study

Part 1: Example situation

In my role I meet many managers and leaders who are suffering from the same problems with delegation. These people often are comfortable with how to set clear objectives. But, when the pressure is on and pieces of work are critical, they find it difficult to answer the following two questions:

1. Should I delegate? (After all, this work has to be done correctly, plus it will be quicker if I do it myself!)

2. To whom should I delegate? (I have only one person who is great at this specific task and they already have a very high workload.)

In order to delegate in the most efficient and effective manner, we need to be confident in our answers to these two questions:

1. Should I delegate this task?

2. And, if so, to whom should I delegate the task?

Self-reflection

- Do you hold onto work because you think there is no one in your team who can do it?
- Do you do things yourself because it is quicker than training someone up to do it (and you really do not have the time for that)?
- Do you have favourite staff who you rely on to do things competently because others in the team just are not as good?
- Are you aware of any of your highly competent people getting bored or demotivated?
- Are all of your team members performing as well they should?

The tools we will use in this step work beautifully with the progressive leadership model and the five golden rules for setting objectives. Together, they will provide clear guidance on when to delegate and to whom. In doing this, the tools will help you if you answered yes to any of the self-reflection questions above.

Tool or model

'Should I delegate this task?'

Our first tool answers this question. The two key reasons for not delegating are:

1. It is quicker if I do it myself.

2. We cannot afford any mistakes and no one else knows how to do this.

Let us explore a typical task that would be quicker to do yourself, instead of training someone to do it well. Let us assume that this task is done weekly and currently takes one hour for you to complete. We could show this visually in a table:

Week	Time we spend on task
1	1 hr

Now let us imagine it is week 2. What would the table look like if you started to train someone else to do the task? For this example, I would like you to work on the basis that the individual you are training has no knowledge of the skill or task (they are right at the bottom of the progressive leadership scale). So, for the first training session, you let the other person observe what you are doing, whilst you explain each step to them. This means it is likely to take twice as long to complete the task, shown in the table below.

Week	Time we spend on task	Cumulative time we have spent on task	Cumulative time we would spend if not training/ delegating	Time cost or time saving
1	1 hr	1 hr	1 hr	-
2	2 hrs	3 hrs	2 hrs	1 hr cost

Now, on to the second training session (week 3). Here you might let them try the task themselves, but perhaps you work alongside them, preventing mistakes and answering questions. This part of the training is likely to be the most time intensive, so let us give it three hours.

Now our table looks like this:

Week	Time we spend on task	Cumulative time we have spent on task	Cumulative time we would spend if not training/ delegating	Time cost or time saving
1	1 hr	1 hr	1 hr	-
2	2 hrs	3 hrs	2 hrs	1 hr cost
3	3 hrs	6 hrs	3 hrs	3 hr cost

At the moment, you can see clearly that training someone to do the job is, initially, a lot more time-costly than just doing it yourself.

But, what happens as they start to get a little better at the task and need less of your time to help them? In the third and fourth training sessions (weeks 4 and 5), the individual still needs you to review their work and support them but, as they get better, the level of support (and therefore time) they need from you begins to drop, as shown in the table below.

Week	Time we spend on task	Cumulative time we have spent on task	Cumulative time we would spend if not training/ delegating	Time cost or time saving
1	1 hr	1 hr	1 hr	-
2	2 hrs	3 hrs	2 hrs	1 hr cost
3	3 hrs	6 hrs	3 hrs	3 hr cost
4	1.5 hrs	7.5 hrs	4 hrs	3.5 hr cost
5	1 hr	8.5 hrs	5 hrs	3.5 hr cost
6	0.5 hrs	9 hrs	6 hrs	3 hr cost

In the fifth training session in our example (week 6), something important has happened. Although you might still be required to spend 30 minutes supporting the person who is now doing the task, it is the first time you have spent less time in a week by delegating than if you had still been doing the task yourself. Although, of course, you have still spent a lot more cumulative time at this point!

As time progresses, the team member will become more competent at the task. They will move up the progressive leadership/competence scale, which means you can spend less and less time supporting them and checking the task. Even if you allow a whole month of 15-minute checks, just so that you have complete confidence that the task is being done correctly, eventually you will end up showing a cumulative time saving. The table on the next page shows the likely time saving, one year after you started training and delegating to your member of staff.

Clearly, we can see that, although there can be an initial cost in time when delegating a task, eventually you will gain much more time than your initial investment. For a task that normally would take you one hour per week, you can expect to gain an entire working week of saved time, if you delegate the task.

For a half-day task, performed once a week, that initially takes 4 working days of your time to train someone for, you will save 22 days per year. That is roughly one whole month of time saved!

 When considering delegation, the question: 'Do I have the time to delegate this?' would be more appropriately phrased as:

'Do I have the time to not delegate this?'

There are times when you cannot delegate a task but, if you examine the task closely, you will find that these situations are rare (normally for regulatory or safety reasons). A staff member's lack of competence does not mean you cannot delegate to them, it simply means that you cannot delegate to them without also providing further training and support.

Week	Time you spend on task	Cumulative time you have spent on task	Cumulative time you would spend if not training/delegating	Time cost or time saving	
1	1 hr	1 hr	1 hr	-	Initially, there is high additional cost of time when delegating and training.
2	2 hrs	3 hrs	2 hrs	1 hr cost	
3	3 hrs	6 hrs	3 hrs	3 hr cost	
4	1 hr 30mins	7 hrs 30 mins	4 hrs	3 hr 30 mins cost	
5	1 hr	8 hrs 30 mins	5 hrs	3 hr 30 mins cost	
6	30 mins	9 hrs	6 hrs	3 hr cost	This reduces (comparatively) as the staff member becomes more competent and needs less support.
7	15 mins	9 hrs 15 mins	7 hrs	2 hr 15 mins cost	
8	15 mins	9 hrs 30 mins	8 hrs	1 hr 30 mins cost	
9	15 mins	9 hrs 45 mins	9 hrs	45 mins cost	
10	15 mins	10 hrs	10 hrs	-	
11	0 mins	10 hrs	11 hrs	1 hr saving	Until you start to reap the rewards and move in to a positive (time) balance.
12	0 mins	10 hrs	12 hrs	2 hr saving	
13	0 mins	10 hrs	13 hrs	3 hr saving	
14	0 mins	10 hrs	14 hrs	4 hr saving	
15	0 mins	10 hrs	15 hrs	5 hr saving	
The pattern continues, with each week that you are not doing the task effectively saving you one hour. The final row below shows the total time saved by the end of the year.					
…52	0 mins	10 hrs	52 hrs	42 hr saving (or 1 working week of time saved!)	Where the final rewards (return on investment) can be both huge and ongoing.

Ultimately, we want to delegate tasks that help grow the capacity and potential of the team. Giving your team members new challenges, and the training to meet those challenges, is one of the best ways to strengthen and develop your staff into a high-performance team.

This theme has been reflected in a key change in management training over the last 10 years or so.

Previously, we taught the mantra:

'Managing is about achieving tasks through people.'

However, now we teach:

'Managing is about developing people through tasks.'

And this leads us nicely onto the next question in delegation:

'To whom should I delegate?'

There is a straightforward answer to the question, 'To whom should I delegate?' It is **the person who will benefit most from this particular piece of development** or, if that is not possible, the person who has time to do it.

This means we should view tasks as development opportunities, where possible. We should consider who in our team either will learn the most from doing the task, or most **needs** to learn from doing the task. That is, who will be able to contribute more to the team if they have the experience of doing this task? Who needs the practice in this area, or who could we train up in this area?

Not all tasks will be able to provide a true development opportunity but, even then, they can be an opportunity for a staff member to practise skills. Sometimes a repetitive task that just needs to be done can be linked with a new skill development area. An example of this would be asking someone to generate a report that they could create easily but also asking them to analyse the report, or present the information at a more senior meeting. In this case, generating the report is, at best, practice of skill, but the analysis or presentation at a senior meeting could provide genuine development opportunities.

Two quick ways to turn mundane tasks into development opportunities are:

1. Delegate the task and also ask the individual to analyse how it could be done better or more efficiently in the future.

2. Delegate the task and also ask the individual to create training documentation so that someone else could do it.

Where there is simply no practice needed and no opportunities for development, work should be assigned fairly across the team. Fairly does not mean equally. Fairly means ensuring everyone is working at roughly the same capacity, so looking at workloads and deciding who best can handle the extra task is key. Be careful here, though. An easy mistake is to find that you are using the same people again and again for the same tasks. If this happens, you will not be gaining much development within the team.

Where possible, use the progressive leadership model to help you decide to whom you should delegate which task.

Level of competency (stage)	Description	Delegate tasks that:
Stage 1	New to task, role or project	Gently progress their level of competency, for example, practise (repetitive) tasks.
Stage 2	Good basic understanding of task, role or project	Allow them to practise their skills, but also ones that challenge and deepen their level of understanding, knowledge and skill.
Stage 3	High level of understanding of task, role or project	Require a high level of skill in this area, but also start to introduce new types of task that may place the individual in stage 1 or stage 2. Your aim here is to continue to develop them to stage 4 in one area, but also to start developing the individual in other areas. A good task to delegate to people in this stage is the training of others who are currently in stage 1.

Level of competency (stage)	Description	Delegate tasks that:
Stage 4	Highly skilled at task, role or project	Are challenging and link to new skills or situations. Your aim here is to help the individual progress to their next career goal, whilst ensuring good succession planning. Give the person new projects and new opportunities. Ask them to project manage a team or write operational training tools for their area of expertise. The most common task to delegate here is the management of other people. But be sure to train them for this new task! Remember, no matter how good they are at their normal job role, if they have never managed anyone before, they will be at stage 1 with regards to the competency of management and leadership.

Case study

Part 2: How the example situation was resolved

In our example situation we looked at two questions:

- 'Should I delegate this?'
- 'If so, to whom?'

The concept that you should be developing the skills of your team constantly suggests that, where possible, the answer is yes, you probably should delegate this task.

When managers tell me they do not have time to delegate because it is quicker to do the task themselves, I ask them to fill in the table that you (hopefully) completed earlier in this step. Then I ask three quick questions:

1. How long will it take you to train this person until they can do the task?

2. Once they can do the task, how much of your time will this free up per year?

3. If you free up more time than it takes to train them, then should you be doing it yourself or delegating that task and training them to do it?

Viewing the task to be delegated as an opportunity for development or practice, as well as using the progressive leadership model to analyse who should do the task, will enable you to decide to whom to delegate the task.

 Exercise

How to use this tool in your own situation

Identify as many of your regular daily, weekly or monthly tasks as you can and list them in the table below. Then analyse and decide who would benefit from being developed through each task. Use the progressive leadership tool to help you do this.

Task	Can I delegate it? Yes/no	Who would benefit most from doing this task?	Why?

Check the tasks that you indicated could not be delegated. Ask yourself:

- Why not?
- How could I overcome that?
- What would the benefit be? (For example, time saved, individual developed.)

Call to action

Answer the following questions honestly. If you are working with a learning group, then share the answers.

- Where are your key staff on the progressive leadership model competency scale?
- What type of tasks do you need to delegate to each individual?
- What tasks have you been holding onto because you think it is quicker if you do them yourself?
- Are tasks distributed fairly in your team? Or do some team members seem to do a lot more of the boring tasks while others do the more exciting and interesting ones?
- What will happen if you delegate tasks effectively and tasks are proactively used to develop people?
- What will be the benefit or reward to you if your team are all highly skilled at multiple types of task?
- How much time could you save over the next year if you delegated your top five repetitive tasks that, currently, you think only you can do?

In one sentence

Managing is not about achieving tasks through people, it is about developing people through tasks.

 You can view a podcast that summarises the main points of this step at:

www.thebusinessgym.net

Step 7

Motivating and engaging people

After reading this step you will:

- Have a clear idea of how to motivate teams and individuals in everyday work
- Understand a simple but powerful leadership technique for increasing engagement.

Case study

Part 1: Example situation

Motivation and engagement have a powerful effect on performance. For a long time this was believed to be true and recently has been proven to be true.[1] If people are motivated and engaged, they will make fewer mistakes, do more work, show greater initiative and produce higher quality work. If people are not motivated and engaged, they are likely to work less, make more mistakes, use less initiative when encountering difficulties or opportunities for improvement and produce lower quality work than people who are motivated and engaged.

Here are some common statements and problems often voiced by business leaders when discussing the motivation of their staff. Perhaps you might recognise some of the statements or problems indicated:

- 'I give them a bonus but all they do is complain that it is not as big as last year's. They should be grateful and motivated by the bonus, but it seems to have the opposite effect!'
- 'People just do not care about the work. They do it because they have to do it, not because they want to do it.'
- 'I cannot motivate my staff because this is a boring, repetitive task. I cannot expect them to be motivated; I wouldn't be if I had to do it.'
- 'Some of my team are really enthusiastic, but some you just cannot motivate. They clearly do not want to be there (at work) and I just wish we could get rid of them.'
- 'Why should I have to motivate people? I am self-motivated and I expect others to be as well!'

---

[1] There have been a number of experiments that have linked motivation and engagement with productivity. As part of a research project for my master's degree in Business Psychology, I explored what happens to productivity when people are engaged with change as opposed to when it is forced upon them. Preliminary results have shown that productivity rises by approximately 25 per cent when staff are correctly motivated and engaged in a task.

Self-reflection

Consider your own team. Who is motivated and who is not? Try mapping your team on the scale below.

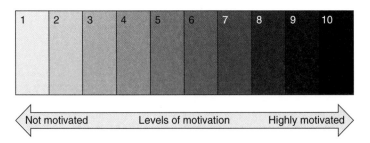

- How do you feel about these different people?
- What would happen if everyone was as motivated as your most motivated member of staff?
- Now consider your own level of motivation: how motivated are you?

Tool or model

To solve the common problems encountered by most leaders and understand how to motivate people, we will use the V3CR model. The V3CR model simply states that, whenever you delegate a task or need to motivate your staff (or yourself), consider the following five points:

1. **Value** – we all need to see value in what we are doing.
2. **Challenge** – everyone needs a challenge in what they do and everyone has a slightly different sense of what is challenging.
3. **Control** – if we feel in control of what we are doing, we are more likely to be engaged and motivated whilst doing it.
4. **Community** – humans are social animals (even antisocial humans!). People are more motivated when they feel part of something.
5. **Recognition** – everyone needs recognition for a task or job well done.

These five points are all linked and connected. They are separated in the V3CR exercise only for the sake of clarity and focus.

We will now explore the five key areas in more detail.

Value

Consider these two statements:

1. 'I need you to run this report.'
2. 'I need you to run this report so that we can have clear idea of how we are progressing. This will help us decide if we need to add more resources or change our plans.'

Statement 2 is likely to be far more motivating because the individual running the report can see the value of what they are doing. In this situation, the person running the report knows why they are running it, i.e. how their work will tie in to a larger objective. This is the very simplest form of value. Knowing why we are doing something not only helps us to do it right, it also helps us to be engaged and motivated when we are doing it.

A few years ago, I did a lot of work with finance teams in the NHS. At the time, they were very demotivated and could not see any real value in the job they were doing. By asking them the following questions, my team were able to build motivation and engagement (and productivity) quickly within the departments. Here is an approximate transcript of some of the conversations we had.

Question – If you did not do your job, what would happen within your hospital or trust?

Answer – The doctors, nurses and consultants would not know what money they have spent and what was remaining.

Question – And what impact would that have on the medical care departments?

Answer – They would mis-spend their budgets (money), run out of money too quickly or not be aware of what resources (money) were available to them. It could also affect how they requested funding for the next year.

Question – And what impact would all of that have on patients?

Answer – It would be disastrous. It would probably mean that people did not get treated or get the medicines they needed. There is never enough money in the NHS, so how it is managed is critical to treating as many patients as possible. Without careful financial management, we cannot run the service effectively.

Question – So does what you do impact patient care?

Answer – Yes, definitely.

Question – Would it be fair to say a hospital or any NHS trust that has good financial management will save more lives?

Answer – Yes.

This exchange may seem very obvious, but that is because hindsight is a wonderful thing. If a member of staff does not know or understand the value of what they are doing, do not expect them to be engaged or motivated when doing it. Luckily, this level of value is easy to clarify, simply ask the individual, 'What is the impact of the task or job that you are doing? How does it help our organisation?' If your member of staff does not know the answer, be sure to explain and discuss it with them. If neither of you can identify why a task needs to be done, other than 'Because we have always done it', then you should, probably, question whether the task should even be done!

Value can also apply differently to people, based on their individual personalities and combined reflective tool (CRT) styles. People find personal value in different ways. For example:

- **Friends** will find additional value in a task if they can see how it will help others.
- **Experts** will find additional value in a task if they can see how it well help to solve a technical, process or system-related problem.
- **Socialites** will find additional value in a task if it is new, exciting or can make themselves and their team look good.
- **Challengers** will find additional value in a task if it is a challenge, competitive or just plain difficult to achieve.

In conclusion, when considering value, ensure that:

- everyone is clear on how their work impacts the organisation or bigger picture, i.e. why it is being done, and great way to do this is to link the task or job to the organisational goals, mission or vision
- an individual value point is identified, such as, 'This will help people', 'This will solve a problem', 'This will make us look great' or 'This is going to be a difficult challenge'.

If this is done correctly, we can start to motivate people when they are doing even the most mundane or undesirable tasks.

Challenge

Everyone needs a certain level of challenge in their work, because challenge is a stimulus.

Occasionally, I ask individuals in my leadership groups to raise their hands if they would (hypothetically) like me to remove all stress and challenge from their environments. In a room of 12 company leaders, normally at least 2 or 3 will raise their hands and say, 'That would be lovely.'

However, removing stimulus and challenge has long been known to be an effective punishment and, even, torture for people. Imagine yourself locked in a grey room, with no windows, no electrical devices (TV, laptop, radio, etc.), no conversation, the same food every day and only water to drink. If your job or life is particularly stressful, then this idea might be appealing for an hour, perhaps even a day. But, spend much longer in this environment without stimulus, and people start to become very depressed. Eventually, madness and hallucinations can start to happen, because the human brain desperately needs some form of stimulation. People need stimulus; we all need a bit of a challenge!

When people raise their hands and say, 'Yes, I would like you to remove all stress and challenge from my job,' what they really mean is that they have too much challenge at the moment. This leads us to the rather obvious conclusion that everyone needs a challenge, but that the challenge should not be unrealistic.

If the challenge is too great, we feel lost, useless and bound to fail. If the challenge is too little, then we become bored, demotivated and we will even attribute less value to what we are doing. The right level of challenge, however, will help an individual stay focused and excited by the task in hand.

We can use tools such as the progressive leadership model and CRT to help identify the correct level of challenge for any individual. Ideally, a task or job should stretch an individual, but not so much that they break. In general, challengers like to be pushed harder than friends. And everyone wants to slowly move along the progressive leadership scale of competence. The figure below can help us see how stress and challenge affects productivity. In the figure the word *eustress* means good stress. It comes from the Greek prefix eu- meaning well or good.

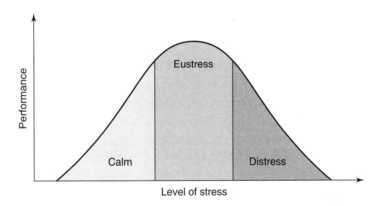

Too little stress or challenge and people become bored and inattentive, mistakes can happen easily and there is little or no perceived value in the task. Too much stress or challenge can lead to being flustered, making mistakes (because too many things are competing for your attention) and, ultimately, burnout or, even, a breakdown.

'But what about the people who don't want a challenge? They reject all offers of training and do not like new ideas!'

Occasionally, you might encounter someone who completely rejects the idea of any kind of challenge or progression at work. They may say that they, 'do not want to grow, learn or be challenged', they 'just want a quiet life'. Be aware that this is a self-defence mechanism. If someone tells you they are happy doing the bare minimum and never being promoted or challenged, watch their face while they say this. They will not be smiling. They may say they are happy, but their facial expression and tone of voice will indicate that they are definitely not.

This defence mechanism is likely to have one of two possible drivers:

1. Either they have more than enough challenge and stress at home and so they do not believe that they can handle any at work; or

2. They believe that if they are challenged they will fail. The most common cause of this belief is someone having low self-esteem and confidence, either because they have tried and failed in the past, they have been bullied and made to feel stupid by managers in the past, or they have a form of learning difficulty, such as dyslexia, which has undermined their confidence.

People who state that they do not want to grow or have any kind of challenge are famously difficult to manage and motivate. However, I have found that setting a gentle challenge, providing lots of support and giving lots of recognition for any success is a sure-fire way of building someone's confidence and self-esteem. It may take patience on behalf of the leader, but it is time well spent when we can turn the unhappy and prickly complainer into a happy, motivated, confident achiever.

'But the job that I am asking people to do is a repetitive and boring job, there is no implicit challenge'

In this situation, your task is to create a challenge. Here are some useful ways that you can create a challenge with tasks that do not seem to have any challenge associated with them:

- How can you do it faster?
- How can you do it to a higher standard of quality?
- What is the easiest way that you can do this whilst maintaining standards and keeping stakeholders happy?
- Can you review the process and find how to do it better?

- Can you do the task and then report on it to others? (The more senior the people we are reporting to, the more of a perceived challenge.)
- Can you identify the most common problems in the process and identify ways to fix them?
- Can you find additional tasks that are linked to this one, for which you could also take responsibility?

Using these questions, we have motivated road builders, administrators and facilities staff (cleaners) to find a challenge in what they do. In each case, the leader had explained that their staff could not be motivated (often using some very derogatory, descriptive language). In each case, identifying the appropriate challenge has led to happier, motivated staff and an increase in productivity, either through getting more done, or improving the standards and quality of what is done.

In conclusion, when considering challenge ensure that:

- every task or job has an element of challenge associated with it
- the level of challenge is appropriate for the individual.

Control

Perceived control is also vital to motivation and it links directly with the concepts of value and challenge. Consider these two scenarios:

1. You do a task but have no control (or say) in how it is done and when it is done.

2. You do a task and are consulted first on how it should be done and when it should be done.

Which of these two scenarios would you find to be the most motivating?

Most people will be much more motivated in the second scenario, because they feel they have input into the task. This increases both their own sense of value or worth and also the level of personal challenge associated with the task.

A common mistake with inexperienced leaders is the perception that a task simply has to be done in a certain way and at a certain time, in order to meet a business need – for example, a report that needs to be generated in Excel every Monday morning for a 10.00 am review meeting. However, the manager can pass perceived control of this task to a member of staff simply by setting the challenge and making the end objectives clear. This is particularly useful and valuable for staff who are competent (at stage 2 or above in the progressive leadership model). Consider these two ways of describing or setting a task:

1. I need you to generate this report by 9.00 am on Monday. Make sure the output is in an Excel spreadsheet.

2. I would like you to take control of generating information that is needed for a meeting that happens at 10.00 am on Monday. The information needs to be very up-to-date, include the weekend sales figures and is critical for decision making in the meeting. Traditionally, it has been presented as an Excel spreadsheet. Have a think about it and let me know when and how you think it will be best to generate the report, please.

In the second scenario, the staff member has been invited to provide input into the how and when of generating the report. They may still generate it at 9.00 am and in Excel. However, they have chosen to do this – they perceive it as within their control.

Interestingly, when using the second technique, often you will find that the staff member makes improvements to the original plan. The example above is a very real one taken from a large insurance company that I worked with. The company needed to run reports for meetings across different regions within the UK. Here are some of the real ways of running the report that staff came up with when they felt they were in control of the task:

- About half the staff generated the report at 9.00 am. The output was in Excel.

- One member of staff came in early (of their own free will) and generated the report at 8.30 am. Because they felt more motivated and responsible for the report, they put in extra effort to ensure it was done absolutely correctly. The output was in Excel.

- One member of staff generated the majority of the report on a Friday evening and then ran an update on Monday morning at 9.00 am. The output was in Excel.
- One member of staff came in early to generate the report at 8.30 am. The output was in Excel, but key trends were also picked out and highlighted. This information was presented using two PowerPoint slides. In the meeting, when the report was presented, people commented on how useful it was to see the information displayed in that manner.

People generating the report were later asked to share their ideas in a cross-regional video conference. During the conference, all of the staff chose to adopt the last method as a company standard for this type of report across all regions. This innovation would not have happened if control had not been passed to the staff generating the report.

Hopefully, by now, you are seeing how value, challenge and control fit in perfectly with everything else that has been explored in this book. If you give your staff a chance to improve things, normally they will!

In conclusion, when considering control ensure that:

- You pass as much control of a task to an individual as you can, whilst ensuring that you do not just abandon them and are not overloading them.

 There is an old army saying about leadership that I have taught and found very useful when considering control: 'Eyes on, but hands off.'

Community

Community builds further on the themes of value, challenge and control. The motivational principle of community states that people like to feel part of something.

By building a sense of community within your teams, staff:

- will find extra value in what they do ('I am helping us all to work towards a common goal.')

- will feel challenged automatically to improve things and do their best ('I am part of something and others are depending on me.')
- are more likely to feel in control of what they do ('We own this, we are responsible.').

Build a sense of community by having team meetings, discussing the ultimate goal or vision of the team, identifying what value the team's work has to the organisation as a whole and asking the team how they could improve things or do things better. In the V3CR model, community and value are almost the same thing. They are separated in the model only to try to give greater clarity. Remember, community does not mean that everyone needs to socialise with each other, listen to each other's problems and hug a lot. Community simply means that people need to feel that they are part of something bigger than just the project or task they are working on.

In conclusion, when considering community ensure that:

- staff feel that they are part of one
- staff feel they are part of something bigger than just the project or task that is immediately in front of them
- you allow staff to share and discuss their ideas together
- the team has a clear common goal or vision that they can all work towards.

Recognition

If someone gets recognition for a job well done, they will be more motivated to do a good job again in the future. In contrast, if they do not receive recognition, they will be demotivated and performance will start to drop. You have probably experienced this already in your own career. The best managers or leaders gave you recognition and kept you motivated; the worst managers or leaders did not and this had a number of knock-on effects, including low morale and motivation, loss of self-esteem and a lack of direction. The very worst thing a leader can do with regards to recognition is steal it, i.e. take credit for someone else's idea, get the recognition from their peer group and pretend that the member of staff had nothing to do with it. I have seen two extreme situations where this actually led to the staff member proactively sabotaging their own ideas and hard work, just so that the leader who was taking credit for it looked stupid.

The biggest mistakes made around recognition are how it is given.

Bonuses and financial rewards are ineffective forms of recognition.

This is a bold statement and it is counterintuitive, but it is backed up by lots of research. We can identify what exactly is going on here with a simple thought experiment.

Suppose I have just given you a bonus of £1,000 for your work this year. Your initial response is likely (but not definitely) to be positive. Now consider the following situations and think about how motivating or demotivating this bonus would be to you:

1. You have received the same bonus of £1,000 each year for the last three years.

2. Last year's bonus was £2,000.

3. You are aware that the average bonus in your team was £2,000 whilst you received only £1,000.

4. The work that you have done this year made £100,000 (or more) for the company.

5. Inflation and your living costs have meant that your expenses have gone up by £5,000 this year.

6. Finally, consider how long it would take you to spend or assign £1,000.

In each of the situations, it does not take long for the bonus to stop being a motivator and actually become a demotivator.

1. In the first situation, the bonus is now expected. It has stopped being a motivator and is now just seen as something that is your due.

2. In the second situation, the bonus has now become an insult and active demotivator. 'If I received a larger bonus last year, why have I got a smaller one this year? Have I done something wrong? Why am I being punished?'

3. In the third situation, again the bonus has actually become insulting and demotivating. How insulting will depend on how you feel about the rest of your team and the work that they have been doing.

4. In the fourth situation, the bonus has become a demotivator because you know the work that you have done is worth far more than £1,000. You are likely to have a positive response initially, but it will sour quite quickly when you consider situation 5.

5. In the fifth situation, the bonus has not reflected inflation or your increased living expenses; it feels like you are going backwards. In this situation, you are likely to consider browsing the job ads for roles that have a higher salary than the one you are on at the moment. You may not actually leave your job but, even considering a move, shows how demotivating the bonus has become.

6. In the sixth situation, we can see that, even if a bonus has a short-term motivating effect, this effect is quickly diminished by real-world demands.

These points do not mean you should never bother paying bonuses, but they do mean that you should never rely on a bonus to be a key motivator.

How should we give recognition?

There are a few ways that we can give effective recognition. First, let us explore how. Despite what we have just found out about bonuses, they can be used as a form of recognition and motivation.

There are two ways that we can use bonuses to give recognition:

1. A simple profit-share system. Companies that give everyone an equal share of profits have been found to be more engaging places to work in. If you know that a fixed percentage of your company's profit will be distributed fairly to all employees, you are more likely to be engaged and motivated in your work. This model is used famously by the John Lewis Group in the UK and helps to keep John Lewis employees motivated, engaged and working hard. It helps to build a strong sense of community with everyone working towards a shared goal.

2. When their work results in a bonus for their peer group, community or families. This powerful motivator has been discovered only

recently through research into motivation. This may sound strange, but it means that, giving a team of five people £200 each and explaining that the bonus is due to the excellent work of an individual is a more powerful form of recognition, than just giving the individual £1,000 for their excellent work. This new insight shows how the respect of peers can be one of the most powerful motivators and forms of recognition we can get. For readers who are familiar with Maslow's hierarchy of needs, this should strike a chord of recognition (see figure below).

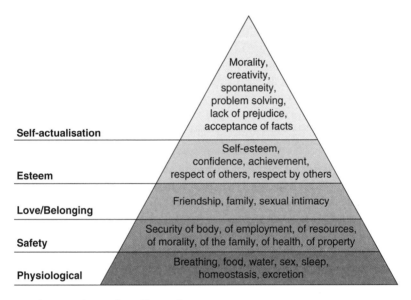

Maslow's Hierarchy of Needs

Maslow, A. H. (1943), 'A theory of human motivation', *Psychological Review* 50(4), 370-96. This content is in the public domain.

Give someone's team a bonus because of their good work and we help them meet all of Maslow's levels; their safety, love/belonging, esteem and self-actualisation needs. They will get an increased sense of security, belonging, esteem (respect from the group) and self-actualisation (from the moral aspect of doing something good for others).

Give someone a financial reward for their good work and you help them meet only two of Maslow's levels: their security and esteem needs (more money equals security and some extra self-respect).

Here are some other great ways to give recognition:

- **Say thank you.** A genuine 'Thank you for the work you have done', is a more powerful motivator than a small financial reward. How would you feel if you got a handwritten letter from your CEO or MD for the work that you have been doing? This is a system of recognition that has a very low cost but a very high impact. Never underestimate the power of a handwritten letter when it comes to saying, 'Well done. Good job. I appreciate it.'

- **A personal gift.** In general, people are more motivated by a personal gift worth £200 than a cheque for £1,000. Equally, a thoughtful gift worth £10, which has been bought with the manager's own personal money, is worth more than a corporately funded £50 gift. While this may sound irrational and illogical, it is, nonetheless, true. There are some conditions, however. The gift should be personalised and, therefore, show genuine appreciation and thought. A company giving out a standardised gift, for example, iPads, will not be perceived as actually caring about their employees. It may be useful here to know that experiences are perceived as far more valuable than material objects. Recent research has shown that an individual receiving a short-break holiday, a day in a luxury spa or a five-star meal will perceive a greater level of recognition than someone who receives a material item (for example, watch, new TV, iPad or games console) of the same value.

- **A new challenge.** If someone has done particularly well, tell them and ask them in which area they would like to develop next. Investing time and training into staff is a great way to show recognition and give the individual a sense of how much they are valued. Promotions and new responsibilities should be given to those who are trusted and who have done well.

- **Give them time.** Sometimes, the most valuable thing a manager can do to give recognition is simply to give the member of staff some of their time. We all recognise that time is one of the most valuable things we have, so spending time with others in a manner of their choosing can be one of the most powerful forms of recognition there is. Imagine if your senior director or CEO asked to spend some time with you because you have been doing such a great job that they wanted to see what you did so that it could be replicated across the company. You might be a little nervous in this situation, but it would be a lovely kind of nervous and you would, likely, be very proud of the experience. Saying to your member of staff, 'You have done a great job and I want to thank you for it. We only have a small budget of £100 but I would really like to do something as a team in order to celebrate and recognise your success, what would you like it to be?' can be a very powerful way to give recognition. The time spent here will have a far greater impact than a £100 bonus or gift voucher.

Case study

Part 2: How the example situation was resolved

V3CR is a simple, but very effective, model. Checking each of the five V3CR points can help to motivate staff and solve most of the common problems around motivation. Let us look again at the original motivation issue that we discussed and see how the V3CR exercise can help.

- 'I give them a bonus, but all they do is complain that it is not as big as last year's. They should be grateful and motivated by the bonus, but it seems to have the opposite effect!' As we have seen, a bonus is only a short-term motivator. Unless someone desperately needs their bonus to survive, it will move from being a motivator to being expected and due, as a matter of course. Depending on what else is happening, it can even become a demotivator. If you have been giving bonuses, you should still continue to do so (you may have a minor revolution on your hands if you announce to people you will stop awarding bonuses because you now understand they are not real motivators!). But, if you want to give genuine recognition, use one of the methods we have discussed in this step.

- 'People just do not care about the work. They do it because they have to do it, not because they want to do it.' Help staff find the value in what they do. Identify why something is being done and how it impacts the organisation as a whole. If, together, you cannot identify why something needs to be done or what impact it has on the company or team as whole, then stop doing it and concentrate resources and effort on something that does have value.

- 'I cannot motivate my staff because this is a boring, repetitive task. I cannot expect them to be motivated; I wouldn't be if I had to do it.' It is possible to find a challenge in almost any task, including cleaning the toilets! If you are really struggling here, then use one of the basic challenges, for example, how can you do it more quickly, better or in a more efficient/ intelligent way?

- 'Some of my team are really enthusiastic, but some you just cannot motivate. They clearly do not want to be there (at work) and I just wish we could get rid of them.' Sit down and talk to the individuals that lack motivation. Do not shout at them or accuse them. Genuinely try to find out why they have so little engagement. There will be a reason! The chances are that you are dealing with someone who has been hurt in the past when they tried to rise to a challenge. Repair the damage by setting small challenges and giving lots of praise for a job well done. Build their confidence and you will build their engagement. Do not confuse a passive, aggressive, stubborn approach with someone who is confident. Humans are normally at their worst when they are frightened or worried, not when they are confident and secure. When people are truly happy and confident in what they are doing, they are rarely prickly, grumpy or belligerent. Remember, even if someone is telling you that they are happy not caring about the quality of their work or what others think of them, their tone of voice and facial expression normally will give away their true feelings about the subject.

- 'Why should I have to motivate people? I am self-motivated and I expect others to be as well!' Whether you choose to motivate your staff actively or not is completely up to you. If you want a high-performing team, you will need to be aware of their motivation and take active steps in motivating them from time to time. Your people are your resources, your way of getting the work done. However, as their leader, it is up to you how much you get out of them. The choice is completely yours.

Exercise

How to use this tool in your own situation

Use this V3CR exercise when considering the motivation of individuals in your team.

This can be planned in private; however, a great way to do this is to sit down and have an open and honest discussion with each member of staff, using the five areas as points of discussion.

The template below will guide you.

 You can also download this template from the Business Gym website associated with this book:

www.thebusinessgym.net

V3CR motivational factor questions	How well it is met at the moment; what could be done to improve this?
Value • What is the value in the work that you do? • What is important to you, personally, in terms of the work that you do, e.g. helping others, intellectual curiosity, challenge, respect for what you do?	

V3CR motivational factor questions	How well it is met at the moment; what could be done to improve this?
Challenge • Are you currently challenged in your role? • Is it the right level of challenge? • Would you like more or less of a challenge?	
Control • How much do you feel your opinion matters when you are set tasks in your role? • How much control do you feel you have when carrying out those tasks?	
Community • Do you feel part of a team or community at work? • Do you feel that your work contributes to a wider goal or vision?	
Recognition • Do you believe you get the correct level of recognition for your work? • What makes you think this?	

You may also want to consider your own levels of motivation by working through this exercise from your own perspective as an employee.

Call to action

Answer the following questions honestly. If you are working with a learning group, then share the answers.

- How motivated are the individuals in your current team?
- What could you do to increase their motivation?
- What might stop you doing this?
- How can you overcome that?
- What would happen to your team's performance if they were all highly motivated individuals?
- What will be the benefit or reward to you if this happens?
- How much time will you save over the next year by having a highly motivated team?

In one sentence

When motivating others to rise to the challenge, always remember: the why is always more important than the what.

 You can view a podcast that summarises the main points of this step at:

www.thebusinessgym.net

Step 8

Giving feedback that leads to positive change

After reading this step you will:

- Understand what can go wrong when a leader tries to give feedback
- Be able to give effective feedback, i.e. feedback that is heard and acted upon
- Be able to give negative feedback in delicate situations, without it being perceived as a personal attack.

Case study

Part 1: Example situation

For any leader, there are two common problematic situations that can arise when trying to give feedback:

- You give feedback around a task or situation, only to find the same mistakes repeated again and again. This means you are having to give the same piece of feedback, to the same person, multiple times, whilst still seeing little or no improvement in how the individual carries out the task. This wastes time for both parties concerned and can lead to a high level of frustration, again, for both parties concerned.

- You give feedback around a task or situation, which the recipient perceives as a personal attack. Not only does this mean that no improvement happens, but also it can seriously damage the relationship between yourself and the individual receiving feedback. In a worst case scenario this can even lead to accusations of bullying and discrimination. In this case, the emotional and time costs are very high. Again, this will be true for both parties concerned. This also may mean that the HR department, senior managers, lawyers and the union also become involved. The cost to the organisation in terms of both time and money can be very high in these situations.

Self-reflection

- How confident are you when giving feedback that could be perceived as a personal attack?
- What worries you when you need to give feedback that could be perceived as a personal attack?
- How often do you give feedback and see an immediate improvement in the performance of the recipient?

Tool or model

To solve or prevent these problems, we will use a tool and a very specific approach. However, before exploring these solutions, I recommend doing the following exercise.

 **Exercise**

Fill in the following table (I have written in a couple of points to help get you started). Try to add at least another 10 points to each side of the table. If you are working as part of a learning group, then use two pieces of flipchart paper, write on one flipchart the heading **effective feedback** and on the other write the heading **ineffective feedback**.

When I received EFFECTIVE FEEDBACK that helped me change the way I did something it was:	When I received INEFFECTIVE FEEDBACK that did not really help me it was:
• Part of a two-way conversation. • Specific.	• One-way. I was just talked at; they were not interested in what I had to say. • Vague.

 Your intentions in giving feedback influence how it will be received by the individual and impact the outcome of your discussion.

First, let us explore the correct approach to feedback.

The best type of feedback is not given it is coached. This is the difference between talking **at** someone, and talking **with** someone. In its simplest form, this means instead of **telling** someone how to do something better, we should **ask** them how they think they could do it better. If the individual you are helping is in progressive leadership stage 1, then this may not be possible. But if they are in stage 2, 3 or 4, then it is both possible and the best way to go. By inviting an answer to the question 'How could you do this better?', you encourage the recipient to think through the task or issue at hand and genuinely identify ways in which they could improve things. You may need to prompt them or offer your own expert perspective. However, this approach is far more engaging for the recipient and will lead to a far better understanding of what can be done to improve things.

When people do not improve after a feedback session, normally it is because they have either rejected the feedback as being unfair or not understood the feedback. If the recipient is generating ways to improve things themselves, then it is almost impossible for them to perceive the ideas as unfair, because they are their own ideas. It also reduces the risk of misunderstanding, as we understand our own ideas and thoughts far better than the suggestions given to us.

The tool used in effective feedback is simple but, to use it for maximum effect, we should always adopt the coaching approach. The tool is called AID feedback.

AID feedback

With AID feedback we follow this simple four-stage process:

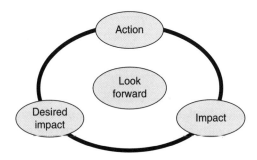

Basic example

1. **Action.** Discuss the particular action that requires feedback. Explore what happened and why it happened. A very basic example of this might be:

   'You ran the meeting well. I would like to give you some specific feedback that might help future meetings go even better. When Bill said he had some concerns about the project, I felt that you were a little dismissive of his opinion and did not give him much time to explain his concerns.'

In this situation we are stating clearly and specifically the action that needs to be improved.

2. **Impact.** Discuss what the impact of the action was and how it will affect the person who did the action (the person to whom you are giving feedback). Continuing our example:

'If Bill felt you were not willing to listen to his concerns, it could mean he is less engaged in the project and less likely to support it as a stakeholder. As project manager, this could make life much harder for you in the future, as now you could have a detractor as a stakeholder instead of an ally.'

3. **Desired impact.** Explore what would be the best outcome for the individual, if they did this task again:

'In the future it is best if you can leave stakeholders feeling positive and engaged towards the project at the end of a meeting like this. It will make life a lot easier and save you time and effort in the long run.'

4. **Action.** We are now back at action. This time we identify what actions would need to happen in the future to achieve the desired impact. In our example, this may mean an explanation:

'In future, if a stakeholder has concerns, it is important to make the time to listen to them. This may be frustrating at the time, but it is an important part of stakeholder management and it will make life a lot easier and, ultimately, save you time as a project manager, because you will have an ally not a detractor.'

You may notice that this technique is pretty much a one-way conversation, with one person giving instructions to another about how they should manage stakeholders in the future. This is why I have labelled this as a basic example. If we now apply the idea of having a two-way coaching-style conversation to this example, our script may start to look more like this.

Adding a coaching approach

1. **Action**

'How do you feel the meeting went?'
'What are you pleased with?'
'What are you less confident or happy about?'

Additional prompting questions could include:

'What was your response when Bill said he had some concerns?'

'How do you think Bill may have perceived your response?'

Occasionally, we may need to point out something that the recipient has overlooked. This is perfectly ok, as long as it is put forward as a suggestion, not an instruction:

'When Bill said he has some concerns and you said, "Oh, don't worry about that. It will all be fine," my perception was that perhaps you didn't really want to hear Bill's concerns. Whether this was what you were thinking or not, is there a danger that Bill perceived it that way as well?'

2. **Impact**

'If Bill did feel that you were not willing to listen to his concerns, what will the impact of that be? How will Bill feel about the project, if he thinks that he has been ignored?'

Followed by:

'If Bill feels that way, what will be the impact on you?'

Again, we may need to prompt a little bit more here:

'Will this mean that Bill is likely to become a detractor or an ally? How much extra work is this likely to cause you, in terms of stakeholder management as you move forward on the project?'

3. **Desired impact**

'In the future, how would you like stakeholders like Bill to react to the project?'

4. **Action**

'So what will you do differently in the future?'

'What will be the pay-off or benefit, if you do this?'

'What challenges might stop you doing this?'

'What can you do to overcome those challenges?'

As you can see, the feedback has now improved from a one-way instruction to a two-way coaching conversation. This will lead to far greater engagement from the recipient and a much higher likelihood of the improvements being made.

Using the AID method of feedback and a coaching approach, it is quite possible to give feedback to a friend above whom you have been promoted, which results in not just an improvement but also genuine gratitude for your help.

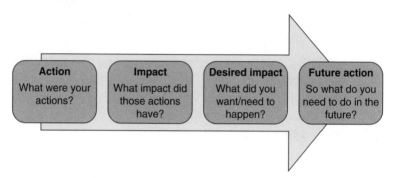

Action	Impact	Desired impact	Future action
What were your actions?	What impact did those actions have?	What did you want/need to happen?	So what do you need to do in the future?

Case study

Part 2: How the example situation was resolved

AID feedback delivered in a coaching manner is highly effective at solving both of the difficulties mentioned at the start of this step.

- You give feedback around a task or situation, only to find the same mistakes repeated again and again.

- People believe what they tell themselves far more than what someone else tells them. A two-way coaching conversation helps someone to explore and understand both what went wrong and how to fix it. This approach is at the heart of all good business mentoring and coaching as well as many counselling and cognitive behavioural therapy techniques. The individual will not feel that the feedback is irrelevant or the improvements are impossible because they themselves have identified the impact (relevance), what needs to be done and how they can do it.

- You give feedback around a task or situation, which the recipient perceives as a personal attack. With a two-way coaching conversation, people will be left feeling that you are helping them, not attacking them. Two-way AID conversations are about exploring how the future can be better, not how terrible the past was. The emphasis is on making life easier in the future by doing a task well, not berating a person for a previous failure.

It should be noted that AID feedback is great, not just for negative feedback, but also for positive feedback. Do not just tell someone they did a good job, empower them by helping them realise that they did a good job and what specifically made it so great!

Giving feedback on attitude

A common mistake when giving feedback to someone on their attitude, is telling someone that they have a bad attitude. Generally, there is no better way of ensuring someone has a bad attitude, than accusing them of having a bad attitude!

Use AID feedback to discuss specific examples of actions that affect how someone's attitude is perceived. For example:

'When Bill asked to do that task, it looked to me as though you scowled and muttered something under your breath. Is this accurate?'

'You are in charge of your reactions and emotions and you may well have cause to be angry or frustrated. How do you think those actions affect how people around you perceive your attitude?'

'How might people view you because of this? What might they say about you?'

'What would your thoughts be if you asked someone to do something and they reacted in the same way that you had done?'

'How much respect would you have for that person in such a situation?'

'How might this affect how you treated them or what opportunities you gave them?'

'How might it affect their appraisal and linked bonus?'

'What actions would you recommend for them to take in the future? Why?'
'What impact could this have on their career and, more importantly, their happiness?'

 Exercise

How to use this tool in your own situation

Consider a piece of feedback that you have delivered recently, where the conversation did not really go as you wanted it to. Perhaps the individual is still making the mistakes, regardless of your feedback, or perhaps they became very emotional when you gave them feedback. How could AID feedback delivered in a coaching manner have changed this?

Plan out the conversation using the AID framework. First, as if you were simply giving feedback, then plan how you could have a coaching style AID feedback conversation.

Direct tell	Coaching style conversation (what can you ask them, in order to help them come up with the answer themselves?)
Action	Action
Impact	Impact
Desired impact	Desired impact
Desired/future action	Desired/future action

Now think about a difficult piece of feedback that you need to deliver to someone. Map out the questions that you think it might be helpful to ask, in order for them to realise what went wrong, what needs to happen and what the benefits to them will be. Remember, when discussing the desired impact or benefits of an improvement, we can use the CRT categories to build extra engagement. Perhaps by doing something better, the individual will be helping the team (**friend**), showing how great they are (**socialite**), getting the result that they want and overcoming the challenge (**challenger**) or proving how intelligent they are (**expert**).

Direct tell	**Coaching style conversation** (what can you ask them, in order to help them come up with the answer themselves?)
Action	**Action**
Impact	**Impact**
Desired impact	**Desired impact**
Desired action/future action	**Desired action/future action**

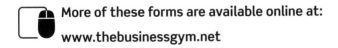

More of these forms are available online at:

www.thebusinessgym.net

Call to action

Answer the following questions honestly. If you are working with a learning group, then share the answers.

- How effective are you when giving feedback at the moment?
- What problems does it cause when feedback conversations are ineffective or do not go well?
- What can you do to improve these situations?
- What might stop you doing this?
- How can you overcome that?
- What will be the benefit or reward if you are able to have more effective and easier feedback conversations?
- How much time will you save over the next year by having more effective feedback conversations that result in real improvements in performance?

In one sentence

The golden rule of influencing (and feedback): ask, do not tell.

 You can view a podcast that summarises the main points of this step at:

www.thebusinessgym.net

Step 9

Moving from being reactive to proactive

After reading this step you will:

- Understand how and why some leaders become trapped in a reactive state

- Be able to recognise when you are in a negative spiral and take action to break out of it

- Become familiar with the two key fundamentals of successful time management

- Have a clear idea of how you can start to over-deliver on your department's tasks or objectives, without forcing your team to work extra hours.

Case study

Part 1: Example situation

'But I do not have time to do all of this!'

In the last 10 years, I do not think I have ever worked with a group of managers or leaders who said, 'Oh, this will be no problem. We have lots of time do this.'

The sad reality is that, if you are like nearly every other manager in the land, you are busy, have a big to-do list, you feel under-resourced and you are not sure where you can find the time to implement all the great ideas that you have taken from this book.

The result of this means you probably find that you are constantly putting out fires or, in other words, you are in a reactive not proactive state.

At the same time, you know that, if you do not change something and implement your ideas for doing things better, you will continue to face the same problems that you have always faced.

'If you always do what you have always done, you will always get what you have always got.'

It would be great if some wonderful fairy godmother could come and sprinkle magical dust and suddenly give you lots more time. Unfortunately (unless you know something that I do not), this is not going to happen. In this step we will look at how you can find that extra little bit of time that will help you start to be proactive and in control, instead of reactive and constantly firefighting.

 'The definition of insanity: doing the same thing over and over again and expecting different results.'

Although this quote is widely attributed to Albert Einstein (*Letters to Solovine: 1906–1955*), it is also widely accepted in literary circles that there is no actual proof he ever said it (one of my reviewers kindly pointed this out to me). Unfortunately, I have been unable to find an original source for this quote.

However, it is such a good one, I wanted to use it anyway. If you know who or where this quote originates, please get in touch, as I really would like to know! My contact details are at the back of this book.

Self-reflection

- Do you feel you have enough time do everything you want to in a working day?
- If you had just 30 more minutes in a working day, how would you use them?
- Do you believe you are able to be proactive in your work or are you generally reactive?
- What would being more proactive actually mean to you? What difference would it make to your team or department?

Tool or model

The two tools or concepts that will help us move from being reactive to proactive are: action management and eat your frog.

Action management

The first thing we need to do in order to help you move from reactive to proactive is to dispel a myth:

There is no such thing as time management.

There are approximately 86,400 seconds in a day (where a day is a 24-hour period). We cannot make more time. We cannot generate or insert more seconds in a day, let alone more minutes or hours. Whilst it is possible to have a very esoteric discussion here about physics, gravity, relativity and time, for practical everyday purposes the amount of time we have each day is fixed. In everyday practical terms, time cannot be manipulated or managed.

What can be managed is **what we do with that time.** This is called **action management.**

There are things (actions) that you do each working day that do not have a particularly big long-term impact on your day. There are also things (actions) that you do each day that are critical to the long-term success of your job role.

Action management simply involves two steps:

1. Identifying what you do that is really important and what you do that is not so important.

2. Replacing the not so important things (for example, checking emails that you have been copied in on; writing the report that no one actually reads, but you do because that is what has always been done; checking your Facebook status; looking at Twitter/news-sites/personal email accounts, etc.), with things that are important (for example, management duties, personal development so that you get better at your job, planning and evaluation, etc.).

A common problem here is the perception that everything that you do is vital. If you believe this to be true, then try this simple exercise.

- If you absolutely had to let one daily action go so that it simply was not done, what would it be?
- Who would die because you let that action go?

If you genuinely cannot think of a single action that you cannot let go without someone actually dying, then please stop reading this step and skip immediately to the next step, **Step 10**: Managing up (or how to say no without ruining your career).

However, the chances are that you can identify at least one daily action that is not critical to your job role, although it probably makes you feel uncomfortable to consider letting it go. Making a change to your daily actions and letting something unimportant slip so that you can replace it with doing something more important feels strange the first time you do it. But what are the consequences if you **do not** change what you are doing?

To help engage you in this action let us briefly explore something called **virtuous** and **negative** spirals.

A negative spiral is one where, because you do not have time for planning and improvement, you continually react to your work-load. The lack of planning and proactivity means we never quite get on top of things and the work just keeps piling up.

People often say to themselves in this situation, 'If I can just get through this project. . .' or 'If I can just make it to the next month when I know it will be quieter then. . .'. This is a delusion. We live in a world where everyone demands increased efficiency, which, in practical terms, means getting more done with fewer resources. If you think your boss or CEO is going to give you and your team a nice break because of how hard you have worked, you are wrong. (Do not believe me? Then look back over the past few years of your working life – how often has that actually happened?) They are far more likely to say, 'Hey look, Sally's team managed X workload this last period. I wonder if we can get them to do X + 10 per cent this period.' The outcome of this cycle is that work pressures build up even more, allowing even less team for effective planning, management and training, ultimately leading to failed targets, a broken system, or worse – a broken person.

The negative spiral is like a horrible helter-skelter ride with spikes at the end instead of a crash mat. It is easy to slip down this terrible helter skelter and, unless you want to be impaled at the bottom, you need to get off the ride.

 Whether you are working in the public or private sectors, for technology companies, finance companies or even a charity, your boss wants you to achieve more output with fewer resources!

In contrast, a virtuous spiral is like a spiral staircase leading upwards that gradually turns into an escalator. It can be hard work climbing up, but it gets easier the higher you climb and the view from the top is great!

A virtuous spiral is one where a small positive change gives you time to make another small positive change, which, in turn, gives you time to make another positive change. . . and so on.

To help achieve successful action management, we can use an Eisenhower matrix.

First, let us create a task list and then identify what tasks are urgent, what tasks are important, what tasks count as both and what tasks count as neither.

Tasks to do this week:	Tasks to do this week which:			
	are important and urgent	are important but not urgent	have a sense of urgency, but are not actually important	are neither important nor urgent
1. 2. 3. 4. 5. 6. 7. 8. 9. 10.				

- Anything that is both important and urgent should be dealt with first.
- Next, deal with what is important but not urgent.
- Anything that is urgent but not actually important to your role should be challenged with the questions: 'Is this really a priority?' and 'How will it help me hit my targets or perform my role?'
- Anything that is neither important nor urgent should be ignored, or dealt with only when all other tasks and proactive planning have been completed.

Tasks can also be mapped out, using an Eisenhower Matrix (see the figure on **page 124**).

 'What is important is seldom urgent and what is urgent is seldom important.'

Dwight D. Eisenhower, Second Word War General and 34th President of the United States of America

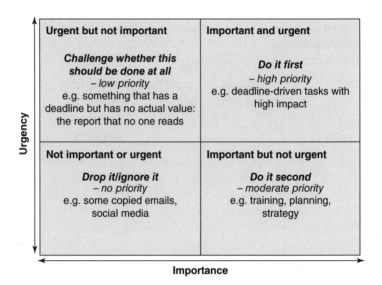

Urgency ↑	Urgent but not important	Important and urgent
	Challenge whether this should be done at all *– low priority* e.g. something that has a deadline but has no actual value: the report that no one reads	***Do it first*** *– high priority* e.g. deadline-driven tasks with high impact
	Not important or urgent	**Important but not urgent**
	Drop it/ignore it *– no priority* e.g. some copied emails, social media	***Do it second*** *– moderate priority* e.g. training, planning, strategy

Importance →

Eisenhower's quote above sums up the concept of the matrix perfectly. This so-called Eisenhower principle is said to be how Eisenhower organised his tasks. The matrix was later popularised by Dr Stephen R. Covey in his groundbreaking book *The 7 Habits of Highly Effective People.*

Action management is the first step of creating a virtuous spiral. The second is to eat your frog!

Eating your frog

There is a wonderful book by Brian Tracy called *Eat That Frog! 21 Great Ways to Stop Procrastinating and Get More Done in Less Time.* The book has sold nearly half a million copies and been translated into to 23 different languages, because its basic principle is simple, practical and highly effective.

Tracy says that we have a habit of putting off the most undesirable tasks for as long as possible. But, if we do the most unpleasant thing first – the action or task that we know we need to do, but really do not want to – then it puts us in a much better mood for the rest of the day and leaves us to get on with our work in a more effective manner.

In reality, this often means we are putting off the important task or action that is not actually urgent, in order to do the task or action that we perceive as urgent, but is not actually important.

One of the clearest examples I have seen of this is people's propensity to check emails that they have been copied in on, before they actually get on with their major tasks or actions. This is normally justified by the statement, 'Yes, but it could be important.' That, of course, is true. The email you have just been copied in on **could** be important, but the chances are that it is not. The fact that you were only copied in and not part of the 'to:' address line is an indication of how important it is for you to read that email. It is also worth bearing in mind that, although the email term cc comes from the phrase carbon copy (meaning an exact duplicate made by using carbon paper), in modern business language the term cc really means covering my ass! If the email was really important, you would have been one of the primary to: addressees. If you do not respond immediately to an email that you have been copied in on, and it actually is important, then rest assured that whoever sent it will call you about it!

 **Exercise**

If you are still unconvinced then try answering these simple self-reflection questions:

How many emails do you get a day?

How many are actually important?

How many are you copied in on?

And, of those, how many are important?

Unless you work on a technical helpdesk, your answers are likely to indicate that checking emails on which you have been copied in, is neither important nor urgent. However, most of us start (to waste) our day doing this!

Emails are a classic tool for procrastination. The psychologist William James said that 'Procrastination is motivation's natural assassin'. So, in his book *Eat That Frog!,* Tracy proposes doing the thing about which you are procrastinating first, in order to stay motivated for the rest of the day.

The phrase 'Eat that frog' comes from the idea that eating a live frog would be a very unpleasant thing to do. So, if you have to do it, you might as well do it immediately and be done with it, instead of having this rather revolting prospect hanging over you.

It should be noted that everyone is different and the world is full of diversity. If you are someone who actually likes the idea of eating a live frog, then perhaps this analogy will not work for you. But, then, if you genuinely like eating live amphibians, you can probably think up your own more relevant analogy that describes the same concept or idea. When I was a child, my dear old mum always used to say, 'Eat your greens first, then they are gone from your plate and you can enjoy the rest of the meal.' Of course, the phrase 'Eat your greens' was referring to vegetables, not live frogs!

 To watch the classic 'Eat that frog' video go to:

www.youtube.com/watch?v=0W7GB5Fh2XM

It is quite amusing and well worth a watch. (Do not worry – no frogs are actually eaten or harmed in any way during the video.)

Case study

Part 2: How the example situation was resolved

In our original example, we were dealing with the phrase: 'But I do not have time to do all of this!'

This challenge is overcome by the manager first accepting that they are correct – probably they do not have time to do it all. So, instead, they need to focus on doing what really counts, and being prepared to push back on what does not really count. The next step in this book will show you how to push back and say no to some tasks.

Using action management means being consciously aware of how we are spending our time and choosing to spend it wisely. Leaders applying the Eisenhower principle quickly find that there are certain tasks or actions that they can delay or even stop doing altogether. This then frees up time to stop, think and actually do something a little more proactive (for example, perhaps training up that new team member so that you can delegate more tasks to them) which, in turn, frees up even more of the leader's time. The leader has now moved from being on a reactive, negative, downward spiral to being on a proactive, positive upwards spiral.

By eating their frog, the leader deals with the task, issue or individual that they really do not want to. In doing this, they stop the situation getting worse and, more importantly, stop the procrastination and worrying getting even worse.

 **Exercise**

How to use this tool in your own situation

First, decide how many hours you are going to work in a day. If you are a hardworking, motivated person, then probably it will be more than your contracted hours, but you should still put a set limit on what is realistic and manageable (*eustress*) and what will lead you to burn out (*distress*).

My contracted hours are:	In order to make sure I feel professional and can show I am putting in extra effort, I will choose to work:
(e.g. 37.5 hrs: 9 am – 5.30 pm minus 1 hour each day for lunch)	(e.g. 43.25 hrs: 8.30 am – 5.45 pm minus 1 hour each day for lunch, plus 2 hours on a Sunday morning)

Second, create a task list.

Tasks or actions I need to do this day/week/month (delete as applicable)		
1	10	19
2	11	20
3	12	21
4	13	22
5	14	23
6	15	24
7	16	25
8	17	26
9	18	27

Third, decide which tasks or actions are both important and urgent, which are important but not urgent, which are urgent but not important and which are neither.

Ensure actions such as training self, training others, delegating, stakeholder management and communicating with your manager are listed in one of the first two columns. These are actions that will help you be proactive and place you on a positive and virtuous upwards spiral. As such, they are **definitely** classed as important, even if they do not always have a sense of urgency.

Tasks and actions that:			
are important and urgent	are important but not urgent	have a sense of urgency, but are not actually important	are neither important nor urgent

 More blank task lists and prioritising forms are available at:
www.thebusinessgym.net

Remember to apply the Eisenhower principle as outlined previously (**page 123**):

Each day, apply the action management principles, and do not be afraid to eat your frog!

- Anything that is both important and urgent should be dealt with first.
- Next deal with what is important but not urgent.
- Anything that is urgent but not actually important to your role should be challenged with the questions: 'Is this really a priority?' and 'How will it help me hit my targets or perform my role?'
- Anything that is neither important nor urgent should be ignored, or dealt with only when all other tasks have been completed.

Call to action

Answer the following questions honestly. If you are working with a learning group, then share the answers.

- What is your biggest waste of time at the moment?
- Do you start your day in a productive way (doing something important), or do your start by procrastinating (for example, checking all emails including ones that are not critical to your job role)?
- What would be your frog?
- What would happen if you dealt with that first (i.e. ate your frog)?
- What do you, personally, need to do in order to become more proactive in your role and more in control of how you spend your time?
- What might stop you doing that?
- What do you need to do to overcome that challenge?
- How will you feel when you are able to do this, and be more proactive instead of reactive?
- What will be the benefit for your company?

In one sentence

Not everything is as urgent or important as it may appear to be initially.

 You can view a podcast that summarises the main points of this step at:

www.thebusinessgym.net

Step **10**

Managing up (or how to say no without ruining your career)

After reading this step you will:

- Understand the importance of a leader being able to say no
- Be able to say no to a request or instruction in a way that leaves the other person saying thank you.

Case study

Part 1: Example situation

- You need to say no to your manager, a stakeholder or a client, but you are worried that others will perceive you as someone who has the wrong kind of attitude.

- You have said no in the past, but it was ignored. The answer that came back was something along the lines of, 'No is not an option, this must get done.'

Being able to say no and have that no actually listened to, is one of the most difficult things an aspiring leader can do. In business we are conditioned to believe that no is a bad word. It shows weakness, a negative attitude and it certainly will not help our careers.

However, being able to say no and be heard is also one of the most important skills you can learn. It will enable you to do a better job, it will mean that your team can function correctly, that your department can hit its targets and it will even protect your organisation and its customers, stakeholders, patients or clients.

It is at this point that we will go full circle, back to the very beginning of this book and remind ourselves of the three biggest reasons that intelligent, hardworking managers and leaders fail.

The three main reasons for failure were identified as follows:

1. Third biggest reason: **promoted because of previous knowledge and skill, but not given management or leadership training for new role.**

2. Second biggest reason: **doing the wrong thing.** Typically, this meant still trying to do their old roles and ignoring the need to actively manage and lead others. However, it also meant being unaware of organisational priorities and working on team tasks that were **not** important whilst not finding time for tasks that actually **were** important.

3. The single biggest reason for a new manager or leader failing was: (. . . if you can imagine a drum roll here please. . .) **'Felt unable to say no.'**

So why is it so important to be able to say no the correct way?

Below are two examples of how not being able to say no in the correct way led to problems for everyone. One is a public sector example and the other is from the private financial sector.

Before you look at the examples, try to answer the following quick questions:

- What will be the impact on you if your stakeholders or line managers do not believe you when you say no?
- What will be the impact if they perceive your saying no as simply you having a bad attitude?
- What will be the short-term impact on your team if people do not believe you when you say no?
- What will be the long-term impact on your team if your no is not heard or not believed?
- What will be the long-term impact on your organisation and on your clients if no one listens or believes you?

I have deliberately used examples that are a few years old now (I have no interest in naming and shaming anyone, and I definitely do not want to influence an organisation's share price). I could very easily have picked ones that are happening right now.

An example from the banking industry

Whilst working with the UK team of a global bank, I came across the following example.

Teams were asking for more resources from a European head of operations (EHO) in order to achieve their project targets. However, the EHO had been tasked by the CEO with finding 15 per cent of cost efficiency savings. The bank was incredibly profitable; however, the CEO knew that the markets were expecting the bank to make cost savings and the share price would be directly impacted by the bank's ability to report these efficiency savings.

In order to meet the 15 per cent target, the EHO adopted the following policy. He would automatically reject the first three requests for resources that someone made. He was working on the basis that, if he applied enough pressure, the teams would find a way to do the work without the additional resources. He also assumed that, if this really could not be done, then the team directors would request the resources a fourth time, at which point the EHO would seriously consider the request. As part of this policy, he also instructed the HR directors of each country to announce a recruitment freeze so that there would be greater control over spending.

In the short term, this plan worked brilliantly. The teams worked extra shifts (without additional pay) in order to achieve the seemingly impossible. The teams looked great. The EHO and CEO looked like they were great leaders and the bank's share price continued to rise as the markets saw how well the bank was being run. The success led to another similar target the following year of making another 15 per cent efficiency saving. After all, this policy had surely shown that, if you squeeze hard enough, people will find a way to achieve the goals?

What the EHO and CEO did not realise was that there was a cost to their approach. The teams achieving the impossible were slowly ground down. Their high workload and stress levels took their toll. People became over tired and then sick (in the most extreme cases they had full breakdowns and major illnesses and then left the company). As fatigue increased, more and more mistakes were made. Each mistake cost more to fix than it would have done to prevent. Every aspect of service suffered, from IT and project management through to customer service. To make up the shortfall of staff, additional (very expensive) contractors were employed. This cost far more than employing permanent staff did, but because of headcount freeze, staff did not see any other option. This short-term focus eventually resulted in customers starting to realise that they were receiving appalling customer service. This, in turn, led to the bank losing a lot of customers.

In the end, a complete U-turn of policy was made. More staff were taken on, multi-million pound investments in training were made and more resources became available. The bank started to regain its market share.

The great tragedy here was that the bank would have been better off financially if it had never implemented such an extreme policy in the first place. The bank's share price actually fell by over 60 per cent during this period, even though the bank was **not** exposed to US toxic loans, which triggered the recent financial crisis.

Focusing on efficiency is important for any leader. But any leader who does this should also understand that it is vital that they very carefully balance costs against quality.

An example from the public sector

I have had the unfortunate opportunity to see the results of the inability to say no first hand on numerous occasions in the public sector. One that particularly sticks in my mind also made national headlines in the UK. Similar stories appear in the national press with alarming regularity.

In 2004, a four-hour target in emergency departments was introduced by the Department of Health for National Health Service acute hospitals in England. Specifically, the target was that at least 98 per cent of patients attending an A&E department must be seen, treated, admitted or discharged in under four hours.

In one of the hospitals, front line staff (nurses, doctors, receptionists, etc.) knew that with the current level of resourcing, this target was impossible. Nursing staff and junior doctors explained to their senior managers that this could not be done and that they would need more resources (staff) to even come close to this target. The response was that no was not an option. As it was a government mandate it **had** to be done. More resources were not an option (there was no budget or, more accurately, political will) and there would be dire consequences for staff, teams and departments that failed to meet the target. Many staff tried to say no again and explain that it simply was not feasible to meet the target without more staff. Again, the response came back that no was not an option – that the target must be met.

Staff felt trapped. They knew they could not meet the target whilst doing their jobs professionally, but they also **perceived** that they had no option other than to follow instructions.

The hospital I am discussing became the focus of the national press when patients were found to have been wheeled into an area to be signed off and then wheeled straight out again to waiting areas and even corridors, with no medical examination or treatment having taken place. This was not done because front line staff did not care. This was done because staff felt they had absolutely no option. They had tried to say no and failed. They felt forced to sacrifice their integrity and professional duty of care in order to make something happen, something that they felt was unachievable in the first place. Let us make this very clear – **people died, because not enough resources were in place to safely meet the target.**

This hospital I have referred to was in an affluent area in the south of England, and it was not alone. The four-hour target led to the many news stories, petitions by doctors, hospital staff and the British Medical Association. Publically, the Government of the day announced that the four-hour targets had been a complete success and encouraged people to vote for them again on the basis of how they were improving the NHS.

As I mentioned earlier, this is not an isolated incident – you may remember the horrific Baby P scandal in Haringey, the Stafford hospital scandal or the fiasco that was the 111 medical centres.

Across both the public and private sectors people break rules and deliver a poor quality of service in order to meet a target, or do something that must be done. In most of these situations a manager or leader somewhere has tried to say '**No – this cannot be done without more resources or time**'. But they have been unsuccessful in saying no and actually being heard.

Here is what usually happens.

Manager (Sam) says *'No, we can't do this with the resources we have'* to senior manager (Louise). Louise replies, *'No is not an option, Sam. This has to be done. The director (*Harvey*) has committed us to these dates now.'* Sam walks away, thinking. *'How the heck am I going to achieve this?'*

Louise then reports to her director Harvey and says, *'We can do it, but it is going to be difficult. Could we get more resources to help achieve this?'* Harvey replies, *'We could, but as long as it is going to get done, it doesn't sound like we need to. Just keep me updated if there are any problems.'*

Louise really doesn't want to tell her boss Harvey that there are potential problems. After all she has already flagged the issue of resources and Harvey didn't seem too keen on the idea. So, instead, she puts more pressure on Sam to ensure that his team deliver the project.

Harvey reports to the client, the stakeholders and his own superior that everything is on track. Meanwhile, Sam gets his team to pull out all of the stops. They work late, cut corners, put other non-urgent things on hold, such as training, appraisals, project reviews, etc. Sam is now in a reactive and negative vicious spiral.

In the end, the project is completed on time, although no one is completely happy with the final result. Sam has learnt that saying no to Louise achieved nothing. Louise has learnt that if Sam says no, he is probably just being negative. Harvey has learnt that when Louise requests extra resources she does not really need them.

In this final workout exercise we will explore, as a leader, how you can say no to your own manager, clients or stakeholders and be heard. We will also explore how you can say no in a way that will not damage your reputation or career prospects. In fact, we will identify how **saying no the right way can make us look good, help others, protect the company and lead to a win/win situation.**

Finally, before we explore the tools that will help us say no in the right way, it is important to fully understand just what we are up against here. In all of the previous examples, someone did try to say no, but someone in authority then told them to do it anyway. In each case, the individual saying no then stopped trying to say no and simply did what they were instructed to do. Why is it we humans find it so difficult to stand up to someone in authority?

One possible explanation comes from an interpretation of a famous (and horrifying) psychological experiment called the Milgram obedience experiment. I have given a brief description of the experiment on the next few pages. If, after reading this, you would like to know more, I recommend watching some of the excellent, but very disturbing, YouTube clips available online.

The Milgram obedience experiment

The inability to say no to a senior person is even more ingrained in us than most would believe. In the 1960s, Stanley Milgram, an American psychologist at Yale University, wanted to see just how powerful our need to follow the instructions of an authority figure were. Or, to put it another way, how easy was it to say no, and stick to that no?

Milgram started his experiments in 1961, shortly after the trial of the Second World War criminal Adolph Eichmann had begun. Eichmann's defence was that he was simply following instructions when he ordered the deaths of millions of Jews in Nazi Germany. Whilst most of the world did not want to believe that a human being would kill another human being simply because they had been ordered to, Milgram wanted to understand just how much of an influence a figure of authority could have on an individual's actions.

The participants in the Milgram experiment were 40 men recruited using newspaper ads. In exchange for their participation, each person was paid $4.50. Remember, this was 1961, so that was a pretty good wage for taking part in a short experiment! As such, a wide range of people were recruited, including academics and business professionals.

Milgram developed an intimidating looking shock generator, with shock levels starting at 30 volts and increasing in 15-volt increments all the way up to 450 volts. The numerous switches were labelled with terms including slight shock, moderate shock and danger: severe shock. The final two switches were labelled with an ominous XXX.

Participants were told that they would take part in an experiment to do with learning and memory. Each participant took the role of a teacher, who was then paired up with a learner. They were instructed that the teacher's role would be to ask the learner questions about memorised word pairs and then deliver an electric shock to the learner every time they gave an incorrect answer.

After their initial meeting, the teacher and learner were situated in different rooms, but with a speaker/audio connection.

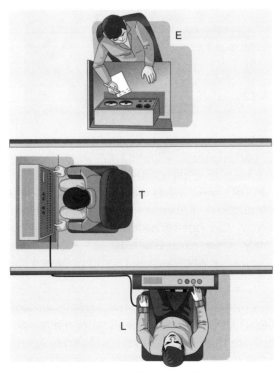

E = Experimenter (token figure of authority),
T = Teacher (the person who was actually being observed),
L = Learner (in reality an actor who was pretending to be electrocuted as part of the experiment)

The learner was first placed in a separate room where the teacher saw them physically strapped to a machine that would deliver electric shocks.

The teacher was then placed in a room with a machine that would control the level of electric shock the learner received. Also in the room with the teacher was the experimenter. Their role was to give instructions to the teacher as the experiment progressed, and apparently record the results of the experiment. They wore a white lab coat and had a clipboard (which were deemed symbols of authority in this setting).

While the participants believed that they were delivering real electric shocks to their partner learners, the learners were actually actors who were part of the real experiment on obedience and just pretending to be shocked. In addition, the experimenter was not recording any results around learning and memory. They were there to act as an authority figure and recorded only whether the teacher obeyed their orders or rebelled.

As the experiment progressed, the participant would hear the learner plead to be released or even complain about a heart condition. Once the 300-volt level had been reached, the learner banged on the wall and demanded to be released. Beyond this point, the learner became completely silent and refused to answer any more questions. The experimenter then instructed the participant to treat this silence as an incorrect response and deliver a further shock.

Most participants asked the experimenter whether they should continue. The experimenter issued a series of four different commands or prompts to the participant teacher. They were:

1. 'Please continue.'

2. 'The experiment requires that you continue.'

3. 'It is absolutely essential that you continue.'

4. 'You have no other choice, you must go on.'

It is important to note here that the participant teachers very much did have a choice. If they refused to deliver an electric shock to the learner, there were no obvious consequences. The experimenter did not threaten them, and spoke in a calm but confident and authoritative tone. The participant teachers' jobs or reputations were not on the line and they were free to leave at any time (although this was not made explicitly clear to them, neither was any attempt made to restrain them in any way).

The level of shock that the participant was willing to deliver was used as the measure of obedience. When Milgram surveyed a group of his peers, they believed that, by the tenth shock, when the victim demands to be free, most participants would stop the experiment. They also predicted that by the 300-volt shock, when the victim refuses to answer, only around 3 per cent of the participants would still continue and, they believed that just 0.1 per cent of the participants would administer the highest shock on the board.

In reality, 65 per cent of the participants in Milgram's initial study delivered the maximum shocks and in doing so believed that they had killed another human being. Of the 40 participants in the initial study, 26 delivered the maximum shocks while only 14 stopped before reaching the highest levels.

It is important to note that many of the subjects became extremely agitated, distraught and angry at the experimenter. **Yet they continued to follow orders all the way to the end.**

Milgram repeated the experiment a number of times with slightly different conditions. He found that changing the level of authority affected how likely people were to obey. For example, not having the authority figure (the experimenter) in the same room as the teacher greatly reduced how likely people were to obey. However, even in this situation, 22 per cent of participants still delivered (what they believed to be) a fatal 450-volt electric shock, because a professor in a white coat and with a clipboard, 'told them to do it'.

This experiment has now been repeated a few times and the results are pretty much the same each time. The participants are not freaks or psychopaths, they are normal people like you and me.

The key lesson to take from Milgram's experiment is that, even when we know we are doing something wrong, it is very difficult to say no to someone who you perceive as having authority. That is, it is really hard to say no to your boss, or any other senior person who asks you to do something, even if you do not actually think you have the time to do it! Finding it difficult to say no does not mean you are weak, it simply means you are human.

Self-reflection

- When would it be good if you could say no?
- How comfortable do you feel saying no to your manager or other senior staff?
- If you have said no in the past, how do you think it affected how people perceive you?
- What currently stops you saying no?

Tool or model

In this workout we will use two techniques to overcome the challenges of saying no. They are the three-stage answer and the broken record technique.

The three-stage answer (or how to say no without saying no)

The three-stage answer is a great way to challenge requests for our time, whilst gaining respect and thanks from the requester. To help set the scene for the three-stage answer, I would like you to answer the following hypothetical questions.

 Exercise

In this scenario, you have approached a member of your team and asked them to take on another task. You know you are adding to their already busy workload, and you also know that it is important that the task is done fast and well.

- How important is it for you to know if the task will be done on time and to the quality you require?
- If this cannot happen (for any reason), when would you like to know about it? Why?
- So, assuming your staff are already working hard and not just being lazy or negative, is it important that they can say no too?
- If a member of your team said, 'No. I can't do that,' what else would you want to know?

When teaching this technique, I have found that the three most common answers to the last question are: I want to know:

1. Whether they have the right attitude and are genuine about their workload, or whether they are just trying to avoid an extra task.

2. Why they cannot do it. What else are they working on?

3. The solutions and options, for example, when it **could** be done, given the current workload, what work could be

deprioritised in order to make room for the task to be done, or a recommendation of who else could do it.

The three-stage answer mirrors the points shown in the table below.

Example

'Yes, I can see why the efficiency savings are so important. If we can do this, it will help everyone. At the moment, we are down two staff due to secondments and sickness so everyone is working at their max. and doing extra overtime in order to hit the current objectives. In order to find the efficiency savings, we need some additional time or resources so that we can do a basic review and figure out what could be done better. Would you prefer to arrange two extra staff for a short period of time so we can do

When trying to say no ensure that you:	
Stage	**Examples**
1. **Remain positive.** Be positive about the request. Show you have the right attitude and genuinely want to help, if you can.	• 'I can see why that is important.' • 'I understand why this is a priority.' • 'I can see why you came to me for this.' • 'I can see the benefit/value if we can do that.'
2. **Explain why you cannot do it.** **Never use the words no, but or however.** People hear these as negative excuses and they will affect people's perception of your attitude. Your reason should be given in a simple confident statement. You are not negotiating here (that happens in the next stage); you are simple stating a fact.	• 'This is what I have to get done by next Tuesday.' • 'The work you have assigned my team already will use up resources until next Tuesday.' • 'I am currently working on a project for Jim, which will tie me up until next Tuesday.' • 'We are currently working on a highest priority rebranding project, which has a deadline of Tuesday.'

When trying to say no ensure that you:	
Stage	Examples
3. **Give at least two solutions and allow the person making a request to come to a decision about what should happen next.** Ensure you place an emphasis on them doing action. Make sure you finish with a question, not a statement – your task here is to be helpful, whilst passing the ball back to the person making the request.	• 'I can get the team to start work on it next Wednesday. Will that be soon enough for you or do you need to find another solution?' • 'Do you want to look at my task list/priorities and let me know what can be dropped to make some room for this? Or are you happy for this to be worked on after we have completed our current tasks? '(This should be used only with someone who has the authority to change your priorities.) • 'Are you happy to speak to Jim and discuss putting his project on hold to make room for this, or do you need to find someone else to work on this?' • 'If you can arrange some extra resources, we can get this done. Is that something you want to arrange or could this wait until next Wednesday?'

the review, look at our current goals and decide which can be dropped so we can prioritise this, or would you prefer we put this on the back burner for now? Obviously, the team are completely committed to helping in any way we can, which is why they are all doing extra unpaid hours at the moment, so we will support whatever decision you think is best. Which option is best for you?'

What happens next

What normally will happen next is that the individual making the request will try to restate their request. They may even try to bully or coerce you into agreeing to their request. At this point, your task is to stand firm and stay both positive and professional. The easiest way to do this is to use the broken record technique.

The broken record technique

Each of the solutions you have stated in the three-stage answer should be genuine and professional. This means you should be very happy to stand by them and restate them. Do not fight the other person. Do not argue with them. Simply restate what you have already said and offer professional, helpful solutions. The broken record technique simply involves sticking to your guns, repeating your professional opinion and trying to be helpful. Here are some more examples of conversations showing the broken record technique being used. Notice that in each situation we are restating what we have already said in stage 3 of the three-stage answer technique.

(These conversations happen after stage 3 of the three-stage answer.)

Requester says:	Your possible replies:
'Look, you don't seem to understand, this is really important and it **must** get done immediately.'	'Yes. I can definitely see why it is important. As things stand we won't be able to look at this until next Wednesday and it doesn't sound like that would be soon enough. Do you want to try and get more resources assigned to our team so that we can look at this, or does it need to be worked on by another team?'
If your manager says, 'Look, just do it, will you!' (This is sometimes known as the JFDI approach, or just ******* do it!)	'Great! Will do. I obviously need to just check with you what we are ok to stop working on so I have the resources to do this. The last thing I want to do is surprise you with not getting something done that you were expecting to get done. What will you be ok with us not doing?'

Requester says:	Your possible replies:
If someone who is senior, but not your manager, says, 'Look, just get it done.'	'Great! I need you to speak to my manager and clear some priorities and then my team and I will be straight on it! Do you want me to check in with my manager in a few minutes or shall I wait for them to come to me once you have spoken to them?'
If your manager says, 'I expect it all to be done and I expect you to manage your priorities so it does all get done.'	'I definitely want to get it all done. I cannot see a way to fit everything in. Please can you show me how I can do this so I can learn what I am doing wrong and do better in the future?'

In the last example, one of two things will happen. Either your line manager will show you what you are doing wrong (perhaps there is an easier way of doing something), or your line manager will realise that it cannot all be done. Either way, this is a positive outcome for you. In the first outcome, you have learnt how to achieve more. In the second outcome, you have shown that you have a desire to achieve and a willingness to learn (i.e. a good attitude), and you were also accurate in your initial assessment. If the second outcome happens, you can also rest assured that next time you explain why something cannot be achieved without more resources or time, you are more likely to be actually listened to.

The steamroller approach to management

This is a style of management that involves pressuring staff into doing things, even if it breaks the member of staff, the team, or creates a long-term harm to the organisation.

Justification: Steamroller managers will explain that they were told no only once so the person probably did not really mean it. They just needed the right motivation.

Solution: Steamrollers cannot be stopped, but they can be redirected with the right question.

Saying no to stakeholders

All of the techniques discussed above can be used with stakeholders and clients. All we need to do is change the vocabulary slightly, for example:

> 'That request seems sensible. It is outside of our initial contract scope so resources have not been paid for and allocated to enable that to happen. Are you happy to pay the extra for the resources to make this change or would you like us to put that request on hold for now? We can always visit the issue again in the future, if you would like to.'

> 'Yes, I can see the benefit, if we had been able to include this in the initial project scope. It is definitely something I will raise as an idea if we run a similar project again and it would have been great to hear about this before the scoping and change requests deadlines had passed. All of the project delivery team are now busy working on the requests that were made in the initial consulting period and ensuring the roll-out happens smoothly and with the minimum disruption. Is this something you feel is important enough to raise a formal request for with your own director so that we get funding to initiate an upgrade project after the initial roll-out?'

Case study

Part 2: How the example situation was resolved

Let us go back to the original problems and also to the number one reason why hardworking new managers fail:

- You need to say no to your manager, a stakeholder or a client, but you are worried that others will perceive you as someone who has the wrong kind of attitude.
- You have said no in the past, but it was ignored. The answer that came back was something along the lines of, 'No is not an option. This must get done.'

The number one reason new leaders fail: **felt unable to say no.**

In the case of the NHS situations I described, being able to say no could have saved lives. If staff had said, 'I can see why these targets are so desirable. We will not be able to meet them without more resources. Can you get us more resources? Should we ignore the targets or do you want us to prioritise targets over the quality of care?' Then a decision starts to be passed up the chain of command. Eventually, someone needs to choose which of these three options will happen. If everyone had done this (i.e. acted professionally and responsibly), then, ultimately, the message would have travelled up the chain and finally arrived at the Health Minister's desk. He (at the time it was John Reid) could then approach his boss, the Prime Minister (at the time, Tony Blair), with the simple question, 'Do you want to give more resources to the NHS so they can meet their targets, or do you want to drop the targets?'

If you are thinking, 'Yes, but giving the NHS more funding is not an option because there was no more money', then I would respond simply that how the UK Government spends its budget is a very complicated political and financial decision. I will not pretend to know the best way to spend the UK budget, but here are some interesting stats:

£109.7 billion	£32.4 billion	£43 billion	£100 billion+
Total UK spend on healthcare	UK defence budget	Interest paid on UK national debt	Lifetime cost of Trident nuclear weapons system

Learning how to say no is not just important for you. It is the professional duty of a good leader and one that is vital for the success of any public, private or charitable organisation.

It does not mean that leaders should just not bother, only ever work set hours or constantly explain why things cannot be done. It does mean that leaders have a professional duty to manage their workload and the workload of their teams in order to ensure that targets are met and work can be done to a high standard, without breaking the resources (i.e. people) doing the work.

The three-stage answer and the broken record technique are the tools that successful leaders use to manage expectations, build credibility, ensure resources are in place to deliver what is need and, ultimately, ensure their team's, department's or organisation's success.

Saying no is not about using the word no; it is about making sure others are aware of what is needed to make it a yes.

 **Exercise**

How to use this tool in your own situation

Think of the last time you needed to say no, but felt unable to, or were not listened to when you did. This could be with your line manager, another member of senior staff, a stakeholder or even a client.

Now plan out a three-stage answer that could have helped in this situation. It may be useful to identify the requester's communication style first (for example, challenger, expert, friend, socialite) so that you can adapt your answer to suit their style.

Stage 1. Be positive.
Stage 2. Explain why you cannot do it (remember do not use the words no, but or however).
Stage 3. Suggest a solution.

Assume that the person making the request would have tried to steamroll you into acceding to their demands and fulfilling their request. Using the broken record technique, how many times do you think you would need to repeat your three-stage answer before the requester understood that you could not do what they wanted (without more resources or time, etc.)?

 Saying no is not about using the word no; it is about giving the requester options for how they can make it a yes (if the options have a high price to pay, then it is up the requester to decide if they will pay it).

 Now think of when you might need to say no in the near future. Who is likely to be the requester and what are they likely to be requesting?

Plan out a three-stage answer to help you manage the request. Again, be sure to think first about what communication style (challenger, expert, socialite and friend) the other person is likely to be using. Although identifying the requester's communication style is not essential, it will help turn this conversation into one that actually helps build rapport and increases the other person's respect for you.

Stage 1. Be positive.
Stage 2. Explain why you cannot do it (remember, do not use the words no, but or however.
Stage 3. Suggest a solution.

Assume that the person making the request will try to steamroll you into acceding to their demands and fulfilling their request. Using the broken record technique, how many times do you think you will need to repeat your three-stage answer before the requester understands that you cannot do what they want (without more resources or time, etc.)?

Given the conclusions drawn from the Milgram obedience experiment, do not be surprised if this is difficult the first time that you do it for real. If you are part of a learning group, then I would encourage you to use their support. Share examples of where this has worked for each of you and, remember, practice makes perfect!

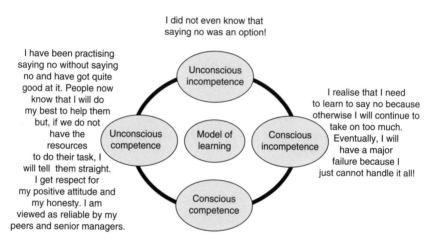

I did not even know that saying no was an option!

I have been practising saying no without saying no and have got quite good at it. People now know that I will do my best to help them but, if we do not have the resources to do their task, I will tell them straight. I get respect for my positive attitude and my honesty. I am viewed as reliable by my peers and senior managers.

I realise that I need to learn to say no because otherwise I will continue to take on too much. Eventually, I will have a major failure because I just cannot handle it all!

I understand how to say no without saying no but it still does not feel natural. I can do it if I have planned out the conversation beforehand but, if someone with enough authority puts enough pressure on me, I will still fold, just like in the Milgram experiment.

Call to action

Answer the following questions honestly. If you are working with a learning group, then share the answers.

- If you do develop the skill to say no and manage your workload appropriately, what are the implications for yourself, your team and your organisation?
- If you do develop the skill to say no and manage your workload appropriately, what will be the benefits for yourself, your team and your organisation?

- What is your biggest challenge to saying no and managing upwards?
- How can you overcome that challenge?
- When will you start using the three-stage answer and broken record techniques?
- How much more effective will you be when you have mastered the leadership skill of saying no, without saying no?

In one sentence

Saying no is not about using the word no, it is about making sure others are aware of what is needed to make it a yes.

 You can view a podcast that summarises the main points of this step at:

www.thebusinessgym.net

Part 2

10 leadership skills in action

Here you will find quick guides for 10 common leadership scenarios. Each guide will help you manage an event or situation in the most effective and efficient manner. Not sure what your first step should be when setting up a new team, or running an appraisal with the individual who has been underperforming? Check out the relevant leadership skill in this Part for instant knowledge and a confidence boost!

Please bear in mind that these skills are abbreviated guides. For more detail, ensure you read the 10 steps in Part 1.

Skill 1

Leading a new team

Where to start

- Start by clarifying or identifying the team mission, i.e. why the team exists. Everyone in the team should understand why they are there, why their salaries get paid, and how their work will contribute towards the wider goals. (You will find more detailed guidance about this in **Step 5**: Setting objectives that work and **Step 7**: Motivating and engaging people.)

- Next, let team members get to know each other. As individuals come to understand and accept each other's communication styles and different ways of thinking, the chances of success increase and the chances of conflict occurring decrease. Use a system, such as combined reflective tool to help team members get to know one another. Any of the common personality tools can be used here, so, if your organisation already has a preference for MBTI, Belbin, SDI, Prism or Insights, make sure everyone completes a questionnaire and then shares the information with the rest of the team. This exercise makes a great team-building event and is a superb way to ensure strength through team diversity. (You will find more detailed guidance about this in **Step 2**: Communication: How to get the best out of people.)

- You already have your mission, but a high-performing team also has a vision and a set of values (sometimes known as its culture). Once a new team has been formed and people have become comfortable with each other and the existing processes, they will be ready to set a vision and agree a set of values. This is a time for you to sit back and be a true leader, not a dictator or autocrat. Your role here is to facilitate the team, developing a vision and values they own themselves, not to have a vision and values forced upon them. Here are two vital questions that you can ask in a team meeting, in order to get the process going:

1. **Vision question:** 'In two years' time, how do we want to be seen by the rest of the company?'
   - If we are seen in this way, what will it mean to us as a team? That is, what will be the impact on the type of work and projects we are handling? How will it impact how we feel about our jobs and the work that we do?
   - If we are seen in this way, what will it mean to us as individuals?
   - What do we need to do as a team to start achieving this?

2. **Values question:** 'How do we want to work as a team and what should be important to us?'
   - Are we all happy to agree that this is the best way for us to work together?
   - What will be the benefits for us (both as a team and individually) if we work to this set of values?
   - Will there be any exceptions?
   - What shall we do if we feel someone is not working within this set of values?

You will find more detailed guidance about this in **Step 1**: Developing the right attitude, **Step 5**: Setting objectives that work and **Step 7**: Motivating and engaging people.

Things to remember

A team is more than just a group of people who happen to work together. A successful team has good communication between its members, who can lean on each other for support. They have a common goal (mission and vision) and an agreed way of working (agreed values, culture or, even, ethics). Above all, a team understands the value of the work that they do. By working as a team, productivity/quality are improved, which, in turn, increases the value and significance of each individual's contribution.

Leading a meeting

Where to start

1. Clearly identify the purpose or goal of the meeting. If you cannot clearly identify the goal of the meeting, do not hold the meeting. Publicise the purpose or goal before the meeting to ensure everyone attending knows why they are there. Ensure everyone invited/attending has a reason to be there and that they can contribute towards achieving the goal. Offer copies of the minutes of the meeting to anyone who is curious about the meeting but does not actually need to attend.

2. Set a clear agenda. Before the meeting commences, send the agenda to everyone that will be attending. Where possible, send the agenda two weeks in advance (for a normal business meeting) and ask if anyone needs to add anything to it. Send a finalised agenda to attendees two to five working days before the meeting. If you are holding a meeting at very short notice, still create an agenda and share it with attendees with as much notice as possible. Even sharing an agenda 30 minutes before a meeting will give attendees some time to think about how to solve the problem being discussed or what information they should bring to the meeting.

3. Even with steps 1 and 2 in place, people will still come with their own burning issues and hidden agenda. **Keep to the point and keep on track.** If people want to discuss something not related to the goal (even people more senior than you), remind them what the purpose of the meeting is and ask if the subject they are trying to discuss would benefit from a separate meeting, perhaps with more relevant attendees. Be genuine, you are not saying this just to shut them up. If the issue they

are trying to raise is important, then perhaps a separate (later) dedicated meeting with a clear goal and agenda is just the right way to deal with the issue. If you are afraid of doing this, then ask yourself – how would you react to someone politely reminding you that your burning issue was not why the meeting was happening, and then **genuinely** asking if another meeting needed to be held to discuss your issue?

You will find more detailed guidance about this in **Step 2**: Communication: How to get the best out of people, **Step 5**: Setting objectives that work and **Step 10**: Managing up (or how to say no without ruining your career.

Things to remember

Millions of hours of productive time are wasted each year in the UK alone, just by holding regular meetings that do not actually achieve anything. The purpose of a **briefing** is to pass information to others, i.e. to talk at them. The purpose of a **meeting** is to share ideas and thoughts in order to achieve a goal, such as improving something, learning from a situation or solving a problem (although all of these, arguably, could be seen as the same thing). With this in mind, the more you can clarify your goal, select the right attendees and prepare them, the more effective your meeting will be.

 Being known as someone who can run successful and effective meetings is a great way to get noticed, respected and promoted.

Leading an appraisal

Where to start

1. There should be no bombshells or shocks in an appraisal. A good leader or manager gives almost immediate feedback on performance; they do not keep it secret for six months whilst they wait for the twice-yearly appraisal to come around.

2. If you have not set clear objectives and goals for the team member, it is very difficult to have an effective appraisal. After all, how can you **fairly** measure how effective someone was, when they did not know exactly what they were supposed to be doing? Ensure your staff member is aware of how they are going to be measured months in advance of the appraisal. The measurement of performance should be as clear and objective as possible. If you are appraising on a subject, such as has the right attitude, or against a company value, such as integrity or goes the extra mile, ensure everyone involved knows what this actually means. Give clear examples of what poor, acceptable, good and exemplary are. The appraisal is not the time to explain these measures; it is the time to ask the staff member how they have done overall and agree what objectives and measures should be in place for next time.

3. Good appraisals involve the staff member doing more talking than the team leader. Ask the staff member to rate themselves against each of the pre-agreed measures and give examples of why they believe this is the case. This forms the start and the basis of the appraisal. If you disagree, then discuss the issue and explore ways to improve performance, for example, support, training, shadowing, more challenging work, etc. There are many reasons for underperformance. Ultimately, you will

find the true reason only through an open and honest two-way conversation.

You will find more detailed guidance about this in **Step 3**: How to build trust, **Step 4**: Adapting your leadership style for the best outcome, **Step 5**: Setting objectives that work, **Step 6**: Delegating to and up-skilling your team, **Step 7**: Motivating and engaging people and **Step 8**: Giving feedback that leads to positive change.

Things to remember

The purpose of an appraisal is to formalise (and make official) how someone has done since their last appraisal. This then leads to agreeing development plans and new objectives (or targets) for the member of staff. Objectives should always – as a minimum – be in a SMART format.

SMART objectives:

- **S**pecific – *what precisely needs doing, what resources will be given and what authority?*
- **M**easurable – *why has this task been set, how does it support a wider goal, what is the significance or value of the task and, ultimately, how will success be measured?*
- **A**ttainable – *in real life, is this genuinely achievable, given the resources available and current workload/skill level?*
- **R**elevant – *why set this task for this individual? How does it link to their normal duties, what will they learn from doing it or get out of it?*
- **T**ime frame – *when does the goal need to be completed and, therefore, more importantly, when does it need to be started by? What checkpoints or review points will there be?*

Leading a conflict resolution session

Where to start

1. Identify why the conflict should be resolved. People need to want to resolve the issue before they can genuinely sit down at a table and discuss the issue with the person they are in conflict with. Start by helping both parties to identify any negative effects that being in conflict has had on them. Common negative effects include, but are not limited to, 'It is making me angry, emotional, frustrated, etc.', 'It is stopping me getting on with my work', 'Not being able to get on with the other person means that I cannot do parts of my job effectively (because they rely on input from the other person)', 'It is creating a bad atmosphere for others, which in turn makes me feel bad', 'It is making me look bad in the eyes of others'.

   Next, help them identify positive reasons to resolve the conflict. Common positive effects include, but are not limited to, 'It will make me happier', 'I will be able to concentrate more on getting my job done', 'If I can get on with the other person I will be able to do my job more easily (because they rely on input from the other person)', 'It will be a nicer environment for others to work in', and 'It will make me look good to others, by showing that I can get on with others and act professionally to resolve conflict when it does occur'.

2. Get both parties to sit down and talk to each other. An effective way to get the conversation going is to get each person involved in the conflict to explain the impact it is having on them and think of at least one thing that they did that may have either led to the conflict or made it worse. The more both parties can accept that they had some responsibility in the

conflict, the more likely they are to see the other person's point of view and reach an amicable resolution.

If one of the people involved refuses to accept that they could possibly ever have done anything wrong, double check the facts and ask the other person what they think the first person did that contributed towards the conflict. This should make a good discussion point to reach mutual understanding.

If the conflict is truly one-sided, then a genuine apology should suffice, with the threat of further action, should the offender repeat their offence.

If both parties are partially responsible, but one individual still refuses to accept any responsibility (when clearly they have some), ask them if their responses and actions helped stop the conflict or helped wind up the other person. Remind them that they are the only person ultimately responsible for their own actions and responses. Then ask them again what they may have done, or not done, that contributed towards the conflict. This is sometimes known as identifying the trigger actions or things that made it worse.

3. When resolved, agree a plan of action to ensure the same conflict does not happen again. This is likely to involve agreeing that certain actions will or will not take place in the future.

You will find more detailed guidance about this in **Step 2**: Communication: How to get the best out of people, **Step 3**: How to build trust and **Step 8**: Giving feedback that leads to positive change.

Things to remember

Conflict normally is due to bad communication and a lack of empathy, i.e. a lack of understanding of how one person's or one team's actions affected another person or team, or why an individual or team acted in a certain way, initially. Building mutual understanding of the how and why both parties contributed towards the conflict is normally enough to resolve the conflict.

Conflict is brought on often by stress or unhappiness. If someone is under a lot of stress or is very unhappy, they are more likely to seek and initiate conflict. This means that conflict is often an indicator of a bigger issue.

Good leaders are aware of real conflict in their team and tackle it immediately. However, they also know an effective team's members will just rub each other up the wrong way sometimes for a short while and that not every little issue needs an intervention.

 It takes two to tango – there are normally two sides to every story.

Leading a teleconference

Where to start

1. Teleconferences are good for briefings, but bad for meetings. Generally, it is accepted that, once you have three or more people in a telephone conversation, at any one time 25–50 per cent of attendees will not be listening or even taking part. For this reason, the first step in teleconferencing is to limit the number of attendees. Even better, meet face to face, wherever it is practical and possible.

2. If you must run a teleconference, follow the same steps as you would for a meeting (see **Skill 2**: Leading a meeting). Ensure you have a clearly identified goal for the teleconference, that you invite the right people to attend and share an agenda before the teleconference takes place.

3. The key problem with teleconferences is keeping everyone engaged. To help with this, draw a diagram of a meeting room table and write in the names of the attendees around the table. Keep the diagram in front of you while you facilitate the call. When discussing a point, **do not** ask if anyone has any comments, as this will mean only the most confident and engaged people speak (i.e. you will miss out on the thoughts and views of everyone else involved). Instead, ask each individual for their comments in turn, using the diagram you have drawn to ensure everyone is asked. Do not be afraid of silence on a teleconference. For example, asking everyone to spend 60 seconds jotting down their thoughts on a pad in front of them before you hear everyone's thoughts is actually a very effective use of telephone time. It may be awkward at first

(no one likes silence on the 'phone) but, if you do this regularly, your attendees will soon get used to it and feel comfortable doing it.

You will find more detailed guidance about this in **Step 2**: Communication: How to get the best out of people and **Step 7**: Motivating and engaging people.

Things to remember

Teleconferences are generally about the least effective type of meeting that you can have. People tune out, disengage and generally get on with other things, such as driving, doing their normal jobs, writing that other report, etc. They are, however, sometimes the only practical option. If you must run a teleconference involving four or more people, your key task is to engage and involve everyone. If you do not value their thoughts, do not invite them to take part in the teleconference in the first place.

 As a salesperson I used to love teleconferences. It was an opportunity to pretend I was doing something that seemed valuable, whilst in reality getting on with a task that was actually valuable – such as making a cup of tea.

Anonymous

Skill 6

Leading a virtual team

Where to start

1. Leading a virtual team follows the same steps and techniques as leading a non-virtual team. However, extra attention needs to be paid to some parts of the process.

2. Just because you have a virtual team does not mean that the team cannot physically come together sometimes in order to do the important stuff. For example, agree a team vision, a common set of values or effective ways of working together. Even if you need to fly people across countries or continents, you will find a good return on investment in bringing the team together occasionally to meet physically. Being in the same physical room, instead of on a teleconference or webconference, will vastly increase the team's ability to get to know one another.

3. To ensure that a geographically distant virtual team functions like a regular team, you will need to put extra effort into making everyone feel like they are part of the team. As well as facilitating a common vision or goal and a shared set of values, try sharing the successes of different parts of the team regularly with everyone else in the wider team. For example, if your people in Germany achieve something special, make sure they get a chance to share this with team members in your American, French and British offices as well. Use virtual presentations (video conferencing) to do this when physical meetings are not a possibility.

You will find more detailed guidance about this in **Step 3** How to build trust, **Step 5** Setting objectives that work and **Step 7** Motivating and engaging people.

Things to remember

Technology is a wonderful enabling tool, especially if you are aware of its pitfalls. Tele-presence technology is coming along in leaps and bounds, although it still has not come close to matching the effectiveness of real presence.

Make sure people know that they can contact you at any time. Autonomy is a wonderful thing, but your team should all know that they have a supportive leader who is there for them when they need you.

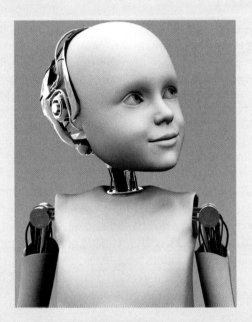

 Tele-presence is an up and coming technology. Unfortunately it can still leave people feeling a little uncomfortable.

Skill 7

Leading a project

Where to start

1. If you are going to lead a project, ensure you follow the rules of project management. In the initial phase, make sure you get your scoping done correctly (identify the user requirement and what exactly the project will seek to do and, equally important, what the project will not be able to do). This is akin to having a clear goal in normal leadership terms.

2. Make sure you are familiar with the following terms: work breakdown structure (WBS), resource breakdown structure (RBS), resource loading, critical path, critical chain, risk matrix and risk management, scope creep. Explanations of these terms have not been included in this book (for word count reasons we had to draw the line somewhere), but you can find detailed descriptions of them online and in other Business Gym books. Once you understand these terms, ensure you follow the wisdom embedded in each of these project management sub-disciplines. Failure to do so is likely to lead to the failure of the project.

3. Leading a project includes leading a team, so nearly everything you have learnt whilst working through this book is likely to be either useful or essential to your success.

You will find more detailed guidance about this in **Step 2**: Communication: How to get the best out of people, **Step 3**: How to build trust, **Step 5**: Setting objectives that work, **Step 6**: Delegating to and up-skilling your team, **Step 8**: Giving feedback that leads to positive change and **Step 10**: Managing up (or how to say no without ruining your career).

Things to remember

Do not rely on a Prince 2 qualification to see you through successfully running a project. Successful project management and leadership take a lot stakeholder management, communication and leadership, not just Gantt charts and resource allocation tables. The most valuable resources in any project are the human beings actually doing the work – look after them and they are more likely to look after your project.

One of the most important parts of a project is the review that should happen at the end. If you do not take time to evaluate what went wrong and why, you are likely to repeat the same mistakes again and again. If there is no time for a review and evaluation meeting, make time – I promise it will save you effort in the long run!

As yet, I have not found a more beautiful warning about project management than this famous 'tree swing' cartoon strip (the original source of this cartoon is not clear).

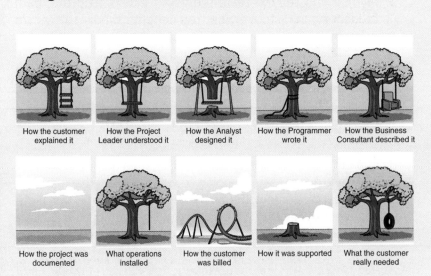

How the customer explained it

How the Project Leader understood it

How the Analyst designed it

How the Programmer wrote it

How the Business Consultant described it

How the project was documented

What operations installed

How the customer was billed

How it was supported

What the customer really needed

Skill **8**

Leading a strategy

Where to start

1. Leading a strategy means being able to get your team (and stakeholders) engaged with the plan and motivated towards achieving the final goal or vision. The easiest way to achieve this is not to tell people what they need to do; it is to ask them what they need to do!

2. Let your team create and own the strategy. First, hold a team briefing and set the team the goal. Second, help the team to identify and explore what the benefits will be to them in achieving the goal. Third, ask the team, 'What is the best way to achieve that goal?' Of course, you will probably want to have created a strategic plan already that you can reference, if the team get stuck. However, where possible, facilitate and ask; avoid telling and instructing. If your team own the strategy, they will be far more engaged than if you just tell them the strategy.

3. Use tools such as appreciative inquiry, road mapping, present state and future state mapping, as well as project management frameworks, to help the team develop a realistic but high-growth strategy that will impress your peer group and achieve the team's strategic goals. Explanations of these terms have not been included in this book (for word count reasons we had to draw the line somewhere), but you can find detailed descriptions of them online and in other Business Gym books.

You will find more detailed guidance about this in **Step 1**: Developing the right attitude, **Step 2**: Communication: How to get the best out of people, **Step 4**: Adapting your leadership style for the best outcome, **Step 5**: Setting objectives that work and **Step 7**: Motivating and engaging people.

Things to remember

'No plan survives first contact with the enemy' is a paraphrased quote that indicates the need for flexibility in any strategy. The best way to achieve flexibility in business is to enable your staff to come up with ideas and make decisions, based upon what is actually happening, as opposed to what should be happening, according to your strategy document. The best way to achieve this is to ensure they are motivated and committed to a final goal and that they have helped shape the strategy themselves. Nothing will enable a team to really understand a strategy as much as helping to shape that strategy in the first place.

'No operation extends with any certainty beyond the first encounter with the main body of the enemy.'

Helmuth Karl Bernhard Graf von Moltke (1800–91), German Field Marshal and Chief of Staff of the Prussian Army for 30 years. He is regarded as one of the great strategists of the 19th century and the creator of a new, more modern method of directing armies in the field.

Skill 9

Leading a presentation

Where to start

1. Have a clear idea of why you are doing this. What is the purpose of the presentation and what do you want the audience to take away from it? Never try for more than three key points that you need the audience to remember. As you rehearse and refine your presentation, ensure that everything you do leads towards that single goal and those (maximum of) three key points.

2. Consider your audience. Ensure you keep the language and explanations at the correct level – not too technical that they will not understand, but not so simple as to patronise them. The same theme of presentation may need to be adapted a lot for different types of audience.

3. Start by explaining (or, even better, asking) what the audience should get out of the presentation, i.e. what benefit there is for them to pay attention. Then use a story or example to illustrate the point you are trying to make.

You will find more detailed guidance about this in **Step 2**: Communication: How to get the best out of people, **Step 7**: Motivating and engaging people and **Step 9**: Moving from being reactive to proactive.)

Things to remember

If you get nervous about giving presentations, then do not worry, you are normal. The vast majority of people suffer from glossophobia (the fear of public speaking or speaking in public).

However, if you recognise that giving a presentation makes you nervous, then you have two choices:

1. Worry like mad and eventually give a presentation that makes you feel sick, even if your audience does not feel that way.

2. Be proactive, stop burying your hand in the sand and hoping it will be all right and, instead, actually do something about it!

Simply typing in the search words 'glossophobia treatment' or 'how to – public speaking' into a popular search engine will give a plethora of options for overcoming your nerves. At the time of writing this book the term 'how to – public speaking' returned over 22,000,000 search results and the more specific term 'glossophobia treatment' returned over 15,000 search results. In summary, there is a lot of help out there. It is up to you what you do with it.

 'Fail to prepare and you prepare to fail.'

This military maxim (with slightly adapted language) is often attributed to Benjamin Franklin and the 7 Ps: 'Prior preparation and planning prevents pee poor performance.'

Skill 10

Leading an interview

Where to start

1. Identify what competencies you are actually looking for. This is not always as straight forward as it sounds and many mistakes are made by recycling the same old job descriptions and person specifications. For example, looking at a typical receptionist job advertisement, you will see that employers want someone with the ability to use particular telephony systems and software applications. In fact, the job of a receptionist is to receive people. A receptionist is there to ensure the first impression that someone gets when they visit or call a company is a positive one. Therefore, the key competencies you should look for when recruiting and interviewing a receptionist are:

   - the ability to make a good first impression (which will be particular to your industry and culture)
   - the ability to make people feel welcome.

   Telephony skills and scheduling software, such as MS Outlook or Google Docs, are easy to teach compared with the competencies I have listed above.

   Once you have identified the competencies, you should find steps 2 and 3 far easier.

2. Create a list of competency-based questions (often called CBQs) and a scoring matrix. **A competency-based question** (CBQ) is very different to a hypothetical question. A CBQ asks the interviewee to talk through examples of their previous experience. By doing this, the interviewer is able to predict how the individual will manage a situation in the future. A hypothetical question asks the individual to predict how they

will act in the future but, in reality, is useful only for showing how well an applicant can answer an interview question. To explain this, consider this real example from a recruitment fair I ran about 15 years ago. In this situation, the same candidate was interviewed by two different companies – we will call them company A and company B.

- Company A: 'How would you motivate a demotivated team?'
- Interviewee: 'Well, first it is important to understand why the team is demotivated. So, I would begin by holding a series of meetings and interviews in order to understand the problem. Next, I would get the team to go through some team-building exercises with a view to creating a common goal and a shared understanding, as these are vital for team motivation. Finally, I would monitor the situation closely to ensure the team are acting as a motivated and unified group.'
- Company B: 'Give us an example of when you have had to motivate a demotivated team. What did you do specifically to motivate them?'
- Interviewee: 'Well, in my last role I had that exact situation. The main thing I did was make sure that they all knew that, if they wanted to complain, they knew where the door was. Ultimately, we were under a lot of pressure as a team and people's jobs were on the line. I just made sure the team knew that! I find the harsh reality of redundancy is a pretty good motivator.'

In the very real example I have given, Company A asked a hypothetical question, to which the interviewee gave a professional, planned and rehearsed answer, while Company B asked a competency-based question, which sought an example of a real past experience. This resulted in the interviewee giving a more honest and less rehearsed answer. Which answer do you think allows you to more accurately predict how the interviewee would motivate a demotivated team in your company? It may not surprise you to know that Company A made the interviewee an offer of employment, whilst Company B did not.

A scoring matrix is simply a rating system for what should be included in a good answer. The main purpose of a scoring system is to help the interviewer make decisions based on evidence instead of a gut feeling (and in doing so remove unconscious bias). Below is a very simple scoring matrix for the competency of good communication skills.

Competency: good communication skills

Competency sub-area	Has experience of	Score
Has been able to adapt communication style, depending on audience	✓	1
Has been able to explain complex matters in a simple way	✓	1
Has been able to engage stakeholders, despite initial resistance	✗	0
Has been able to give successful presentations	✓	1
Total score for competency		3/4

3. Make sure you have someone dedicated to taking notes and recording the interviewee's answers. The best practice approach is to score the answers and make decisions only after all of the interviews have taken place. Try to make decisions based only on the evidence provided, not based on how you felt about the candidate. Remember, the most attractive candidates, the funniest candidates and the candidates that are most like you may not actually be the best candidates for the job! Where possible, seek to remove unconscious bias. If you are not familiar with the terms unconscious bias and Halo effect, it is recommended that you find out what they are before you lead your next interview!

You will find more detailed guidance about this in **Step 2**: Communication: How to get the best out of people.

Things to remember

Probing or follow-up questions are used to facilitate clear and detailed answers that will aid accurate scoring of the interview. A modest, introverted candidate may give a much briefer answer than an individual who is naturally confident in interviews. One of the tasks of an interviewer is to ensure that it is the candidate's skills and experience that are assessed, not the candidate's ability to answer interview questions.

 Interviewer: *'So do you see yourself as more of a circle, a square or a triangle?'*

Interviewee: *'Ummmm. . .'* (whilst thinking, *'This interviewer is clearly a bit of an idiot!'*)

Part 3

10 common leadership challenges

Challenge 1	How do I balance leadership responsibilities with my day job?
Challenge 2	How do I manage a team that is split over multiple locations?
Challenge 3	How do I manage someone over whom I have been promoted?
Challenge 4	How do I deal with conflict in my team?
Challenge 5	How do I manage someone who is better than me?
Challenge 6	How do I engage my team with change?
Challenge 7	How do I appear confident, authoritative?
Challenge 8	How do I stay informed without micromanaging?
Challenge 9	How do I build team unity?
Challenge 10	How do I set effective targets?

Note: these are very fast answers to common problems. They do not replace the full explanations and tutorials that form the steps in Part 1 of this book.

Challenge 1

How do I balance leadership responsibilities with my day job?

By being aware that your leadership responsibilities ARE part of your day job.

Make sure your diary shows time dedicated for recruitment, training, appraisals, giving feedback, process reviews, staff professional development and performance management.

How much time you need to do this is dependent on how large your team is, their churn rate (how often people leave your team and you need to re-recruit) and how skilled your team are. If you are leading just one, highly skilled individual, you may be able to spend as little as 5 per cent of your time dedicated to managing and leading them (that is as little as about 25 minutes in a typical 8-hour working day). If you are running a team of 12 mixed skill staff and need to recruit a new person every 6 months, expect to spend between 25–50 per cent of your time managing and leading them. A new team of 20 staff should take 75–100 per cent of your time for an initial period.

Dedicating this time can seem a little scary at first. However, at the start of this book, in **Step 1**: Developing the right attitude, we explored together how good leadership can easily increase a team's quality and productivity by over 25 per cent. If you are running a team of 12 people and invest 50 of your time into being a good leader, you can expect an average increase in productivity of 25 per cent from each person. That means that investing half of your own man- or woman-hours will give you a return on investment equivalent to 3 extra full-time staff. How about that for efficiency!

Successful companies ensure that managers and leaders have dedicated time to manage and lead their teams. Managers who forget the importance of dedicated time for leadership, or are not allowed to dedicate time to leading, are actively limiting their team's potential productivity.

To explore this topic more you may find it useful to read **Step 9**: Moving from being reactive to proactive and **Step 10**: Managing up (or how to say no without ruining your career.

How do I manage a team that is split over multiple locations?

By ensuring you do not always keep it that way.

Individuals in a geographically split team may not actually feel that they are part of team. As the leader, it is up to you to ensure that they come together as often as possible to meet physically, talk about how things are going and how they can work together in a more effective manner. This should start with the team setting itself a vision or goal and some common values.

You will need to balance the cost and time implications of people travelling to meet with each other, with the increased productivity you will get from everyone if they truly feel part of the team. Video and teleconferences can help, but should never be relied upon. With our current state of technology, nothing beats meeting the rest of your team face to face. People who have actually met are more likely to help each other to achieve a common goal. They are also more likely to resolve misunderstandings proactively, before they escalate to resentment and conflict (two things that can greatly harm the productivity of an individual and the team as a whole).

How do I manage someone over whom I have been promoted?

By being honest, genuine and fair with them.

Do not be threatened by them or embarrassed by the situation. If you are calm about everything and show that it is not awkward, then they are less likely to feel resentful and awkward when being managed by you.

You will need to work hard to demonstrate that you will be a good leader/manager to them. This means making sure you develop them and recognise good work. You will need to show that you care about their development. This may mean helping them to see why you got promoted over them and helping them to refine their skills or professional image so that they will get the promotion they go for next time.

One of the hardest things in this situation is giving constructive, but negative, feedback to someone who is a good friend and that you used to work alongside. For more information on stress-free ways to do this, read **Step 8**: Giving feedback that leads to positive change.

Challenge 4

How do I deal with conflict in my team?

Follow these two rules:

1. Decide if it really is conflict or if it is just individuals in the team letting off steam and sorting out a kind of pecking order. Over-cautious new leaders can sometimes make a mountain out of a molehill. If your team has agreed a clear set of values or behaviours, you should be able to refer to these and ask yourself and the team members, 'Is this how we all agreed to work together?' This is often enough to stop a disagreement before it becomes actual conflict. Remember, it is always more effective to ask not tell in these situations. If you talk to your staff like you are the parent and they are your children, do not be surprised if they continue to act like children.

2. If you decide that what you are observing clearly is conflict, or if one of the parties approaches you with a genuine complaint, ensure you act on it immediately. As the leader, how you deal with situations like this sends clear messages to the rest of the team about what is acceptable and unacceptable in the team.

How do I manage someone who is better than me?

Embrace the fact that they are better than you. Do not be threatened by them. Give them recognition and challenge.

If you have a highly skilled team, then it stands to reason that some people in your team will be better at doing their tasks than you are at doing their tasks. Not only is that ok, it is expected and normal. Would you expect the CEO of a large company to be as skilled with tax law as his financial director? Would you expect the financial director be as skilled with tax law as the tax law specialist that is employed with the specific aim of saving money on tax? Would you expect the tax law specialist to be as efficient at writing up the financial accounts as the financial accountant, whose job it is to write up and present the overall accounts, with input from people like the tax law specialist?

Everyone in a team has a role to play. You may still be doing a lot of hands-on work in your day job, but your core function as a leader is to lead your team. The moment you are promoted to a position of leadership, leading becomes the specialist skill you need to be the best at. This does not mean you cannot be a subject matter expert (SME) in another technical area. However, it does mean you should no longer be the only, or even the best, (SME) in that technical subject. If you try and hold onto the mantle of best SME for the role you used to do, then you will spending time constantly up-skilling in your old job, instead of developing your skills to fit your new job, i.e. leader.

How do I engage my team with change?

By not forcing the change on people and instead setting them the new challenge and facilitating the team to decide how to meet it.

This has been the focus of my master's degree in business psychology. It will also be the subject of my next leadership book, which currently has a working title of *The 4 laws of change*. To help you, here is a sneak preview of the four laws:

- Law 1: Change is constant. There is nothing here!
- Law 2: Change can be perceived as good, bad, or even both at the same time. It all depends who you are and how the change has been introduced to you (see Law 3).
- Law 3: If you create the change, you will embrace it. If change is forced upon you, you will resist it. There is a lot of scientific evidence for this law, as well as many, many anecdotal examples, both of which I introduce in my new book. However, in the interest of giving a quick answer to this question, it is probably sufficient to say that your role as the leader is to set the team new targets, help them explore what the benefits are of having a new structure/process, etc. and what the risks are of not changing, and then help them to create their own plan for how to do it.
- The risks are sometimes referred to as a burning platform, i.e. something negative that will force people to jump to a new platform or new way of working. The most common risks or burning platforms are: 'We will be outcompeted, the company/team will then either downsize, be bought out or disappear and all of our jobs will be threatened', or 'Given our

funding or resources, we will be unable to meet the increasing demands of our customers or patients, ultimately leading to loss of customers, harming patients, being decommissioned or outcompeted'. Notice that the second risk ultimately leads back to the first risk, i.e. we will not survive as an organisation/department/team and all of our jobs will be under threat.

- In summary, Law 3 implies that you should help your team be the change, not the victims of it.

- Law 4: With enough time or use, the change will become the norm. This law is there to reassure you and your staff that, eventually, whatever is scary and new, actually will be seen as normal, as the usual way of working or the standard operating procedure.

- Just think of some of the biggest changes to hit society in the last 40 years. For example, the internet, email, social media, smart phones, etc. These are now the norm and it is difficult to imagine living without them. Google was incorporated in 1998. In December 2013 there were approximately 12.5 billion Google searches (per month) and it is now difficult to imagine a world where answers to almost anything are not just a few clicks away. In fact, in many countries, internet access is viewed as one of the basic human rights!

Challenge **7**

How do I appear confident, authoritative?

This is another subject that has generated many books. If you are really struggling with this, I highly recommend attending a training session on assertiveness, public speaking, presentation skills or confidence. A good course on any of these subjects will help you develop the gravitas and authority that you are seeking. Most of the big training companies in the UK (for example, QA Ltd, BPP, Kaplan, etc.) offer decent courses on all of these subjects. However, a quick internet search will give you many, many options that you can choose from.

A quick answer for the purposes of this book would be to identify what you are good at and recognise that.

If you are invited into a meeting of more senior staff, think about why you are there. There is a good chance that you have (or have access to) specialist knowledge or skills that are needed in the meeting. Be confident in what you know and can do, and honest about what you do not know or cannot do.

With your team, ensure you understand how far your authority stretches and decide early on just what it would take for you to exercise that authority. For example, at what point would you decide to put someone into disciplinary measures? Could you actually sack someone if they pushed you far enough? And, if so, just how far would they need to push you? Thinking about these things before you need to do them will help build your confidence, assertiveness and sense of authority for when you really need them.

Challenge 8

How do I stay informed without micromanaging?

By being clear on exactly what you need to stay informed about and thinking carefully about what you trust your team to do without you.

If you are having problems with this one, then have a look at the progressive leadership model in **Step 4**: Adapting your leadership style for the best outcome. The progressive leadership model is designed specifically to help you analyse when you need to be hands on and give lots of direction (micromanage) and when you should step back and let go.

Challenge 9

How do I build team unity?

By allowing the team to set their own vision or goal and their own set of behaviours for how they will work together.

The behaviours are normally referred to as values. They are an agreed way of communicating and working together.

Note that a team's long-term vision or goal is very different to its short-term target. An example of a target is 'Make £1 million in revenue', 'Answer every internal query within 48 hours' or, perhaps, 'Process 1,000 new applications per month'. Examples of a vision or goal could be to 'become the most respected revenue-earning team in the company', 'become the trusted advisors of choice, for internal queries' or, perhaps, to 'be the application-processing team that everyone wants to work for'.

It is vital that the team sets their own vision and values. A vision's or value's system created by senior leadership and then rolled out to the team will never really be fully embraced by the team and will fail in creating unity. This does not mean that a team's vision or values should be at odds with a corporate vision or values. A team can easily have their own vision and set of values, without those values being in conflict with the corporate ones.

Challenge 10

How do I set effective targets?

By making sure targets are difficult to achieve, but never impossible to achieve.

These are called stretch targets because they stretch the individuals involved in reaching them. The purpose of these is to help both individuals and teams grow, but not break.

To ensure maximum growth over the long term, you should allow teams to relax in between stretch targets. A good analogy for this is what happens in a physical training session at the gym. If you want to increase your strength or endurance, you need to push yourself, i.e. stretch your ability. However, it is also important to give your body and muscles time to relax and recuperate between workouts. This allows the muscles to react to what they have just gone through and make changes in order to meet that level of exertion more easily next time. Or, in other words, to grow and get stronger. If you do not let the muscles in your body rest between workouts, then you will not only stop them from growing and getting stronger, you will actively damage them. This will reduce their efficiency and effectiveness and may cause long-term harm, affecting how well they can function in the future.

Using the analogy above, your team is no different to your muscles. Stretch them in order to increase capacity (strength and endurance), but do not overdo it, and make sure you give them breaks so that they can reorganise, develop and grow.

Never set a target that you either do not think you could achieve yourself, or do not know how your team could achieve. No one likes to be set up to fail and you will notice an immediate impact on team motivation, engagement and, ultimately, productivity/results.

How to work with a manager, colleague or learning group to put your new skills into action

Whether you have been working through this book from beginning to end, or diving into the specific steps or skills that are most relevant to you, you will still find enormous value in reviewing and evaluating your skills. On the next few pages you will find guidance for how to run and take part in a learning review session (referred to as an LRS). These sessions are very useful, as they will enable you to refine your skills, learn from your mistakes and, ultimately, build your confidence in how to use the tools, techniques and methods discussed in this book.

- Is it best to share with my manager, a buddy, or be part of a larger learning group for my LRS?
  - o The most productive groups are made up of 6–8 people sharing their experiences and learning. If the group size gets above 10 people, it is recommended that you split into 2 groups of 5. In an LRS, it is very important that everyone gets a chance to share their experiences, both good and bad.
  - o If you do not have a peer group who are also working through this book, then having an LRS with a colleague or your manager is still very valuable.

- How much time should I give to a LRS?
  - o If you are meeting one on one with a buddy or your manager, you should allocate 60–90 minutes for each LRS.
  - o If you are meeting more people as part of a learning group, you will need to allow more time for the LRS. As a rough guide, for most of the leadership programmes that I run, I will dedicate four hours for an LRS that has eight members in the group.

- How often should we run an LRS?
  - o As a general guide, you should seek to run an LRS two weeks after any learning intervention. For the purposes of this book, that means two weeks after you have completed one of the steps. This will give you enough time to have practically applied what you have learnt, but it will be soon enough so that the tools and techniques discussed are still fresh in your mind.

- What should be the structure of an LRS? That is, what should actually happen in an LRS?

- In your first LRS, you should adopt the following structure:

  1. Get each member of the group to share a success story. This is where they have tried to use one of the tools or techniques they have learnt and it has worked.

  2. Write on a flipchart the word FAIL and remind everyone that FAIL stands for **F**irst **A**ttempt **I**n **L**earning. It is actually easier to learn more from a mistake than a success. For example, as children we can be told not to touch something that is dangerously hot, but normally it is not until we either burn ourselves or see someone else burnt that we learn what the term dangerously hot really means.

  3. Get each member of the group to share an experience of where they have tried to use a leadership technique covered in the book, but it has not quite worked. For each example, the rest of the group should first explore what actually happened, and then offer ideas and advice for how to solve the challenge. Whilst this works best in larger LRS groups, it is still a valid technique for smaller groups, pairs or if you are running an LRS with just your manager. **Senior line managers: you should feel free to share your own successes and failures as well in this session. Help your staff learn by sharing your own experience! I guarantee you will also benefit from discussing your successes and failures in this way.**

  4. Each member of the group should state something that they will try before the next LRS.

- In your second and subsequent LRS, follow the structure above, but start with an additional exercise called a review quiz. A review quiz is where each member of the LRS comes up with three to five quiz questions that they will ask everyone else in the LRS. (If there are just two of you in the LRS, then generate five questions each; if there are four people, then generate four questions; if there are eight, generate three questions each).

Group members should base their questions around anything that has been covered in the book that has been read by all, or anything that has arisen in a previous LRS. For example, 'What should you do when communicating with someone whose personality type is challenger?' or 'What is the trust equation?'

Each member should ask a question in turn and give the rest of the group 30 seconds or so to write down an answer. Continue going around the group until everyone has exhausted their questions. Once all of the questions have been asked, it is time to explore the answers. The group member who asked the question starts by offering the answer that they were looking for. Other members then either confirm that their own answers agree, or explain what they have written as an answer and why. The person asking the question also decides how marks are awarded. Although only one mark in total should be awarded for each correct answer, it is possible to give fractions of marks. For example, for the question 'What should you do when communicating with someone whose personality type is challenger?', the questioner might decide to give a half mark for 'be concise' and another half mark for 'be direct'. Marks are down to the questioner's discretion, so an answer of, 'Get to the point. Do not waffle and try to challenge them in the correct way' could still get a whole mark. Even though it was not exactly what the questioner was looking for, it is still a good and accurate answer.

The purpose of the review quiz is to help embed knowledge and understanding in someone's mind. Studies have shown that, if you are quizzed regularly, there is a higher retention of knowledge. Studies have also shown that, if you generate the quiz questions for others, the retention levels are even higher. I, personally, have found that people rarely forget the answers to the quiz questions that they generated in the review quizzes as part of an LRS, even one year later!

Finally, the review quiz is a fun but valuable way to kick-start an LRS. When running an LRS for eight aspiring leaders, I like to give a token prize to the winner (normally their choice of a box of chocolates or a book). However, playing for glory can be just as enjoyable!

Congratulations! You have now completed the 10 steps to better leadership in the Business Gym learning programme. I hope that you have found it useful and that the tools and techniques covered have already helped you to meet the challenges of modern business leadership.

There is just one final thing to do now, which is to complete your post-workout assessment. On the next few pages are the same questions that you were asked at the start of the book in the pre-workout self-assessment.

Post-assessment

Rate your answers and see where you have progressed the most and where you might want to practise your skills further.

Score yourself on a scale of 1 to 10 for each of these questions, with 10 indicating a high level of confidence and skill and 1 the lowest.

1. How would you currently rate your **general management and leadership** skills? (How many hours a week do you spend currently worrying over whether you have managed a team member or situation correctly?)

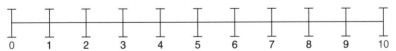

2. How effective is your **communication**? (How many hours a week do you spend currently having the same conversation repeatedly because it was not understood or did not work the first time?)

3. How much are you **trusted** by your team? (How many hours a week do you spend currently trying to get people to trust you, for example, getting staff to be completely open and honest with you?)

4. Do you currently **adapt your leadership style** for different people in different situations? (How many hours a week do you spend currently fixing your team members' mistakes or finding yourself exasperated or frustrated with one or more team members?)

5. How good are you at **setting objectives** that meet your boss's requirements and are met by your team? (How many hours a week do you spend currently chasing team members' objectives/results or putting in fixes because an objective has not been met?)

6. How comfortable or confident are you in **delegating** work to your team? (How many hours a week do you spend currently doing work that deep down you know you should delegate but do not feel that you can?)

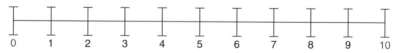

7. How good are you at **motivating** others? How engaged and motivated is your team? (How many hours a week do you spend currently trying to motivate people, particularly the person who is really difficult to motivate?)

8. How comfortable or confident are you in giving constructive **feedback** that actually leads to improvements? (How many hours a week do you spend currently worrying about or avoiding giving difficult feedback or giving the same feedback multiple times because the first time it was not taken on board?)

9. Do you feel that you are more **reactive** (1) or **proactive** (10) in your work as a manager? (How many hours a week do you spend currently reacting to situations and putting out fires instead of planning in order to ensure that problems do not happen in the first place?)

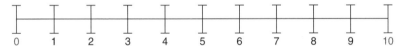

10. How comfortable are you in **managing upwards** and saying no to your own line manager? (How many hours a week do you spend currently achieving the unachievable, working without the correct resourcing levels or worrying about how to manage your manager?)

These are your baselines. Undoubtedly, you will want to check how they have improved when you get to the end of this learning programme, which is why the post-workout assessment is at the end of the book. Each question in this questionnaire is related to one of the steps, so, if you have identified one particular area that you really feel you would like to develop first, you may choose to jump straight to the relevant step. For example, if you are scoring 8+ on everything except managing upwards, you might first want to work through **Step 10**: Managing up.

Good luck!

Nick Winston

Leadership consultant/senior learning consultant/programme manager/change consultant/trainer/coach/facilitator/dad/ husband/person who takes the bins out on a Sunday evening.

(My title seems to change, depending where I am and what I am doing.)

Contact me at: nick.winston@hotmail.co.uk

What did you think of this book?

We're really keen to hear from you about this book, so that we can make our publishing even better.

Please log on to the following website and leave us your feedback.

It will only take a few minutes and your thoughts are invaluable to us.

www.pearsoned.co.uk/bookfeedback

Do you want your people to be the very best at what they do?

Talk to us about how we can help.

As the world's leading learning company, we know a lot about what your people need in order to be better at what they do.

Whatever subject or skills you've got in mind (from presenting or persuasion to coaching or communication skills), and at whatever level (from new-starters through to top executives) we can help you deliver tried-and-tested, essential learning straight to your workforce – whatever they need, whenever they need it and wherever they are.

Talk to us today about how we can:

- Complement and support your existing learning and development programmes
- Enhance and augment your people's learning experience
- Match your needs to the best of our content
- Customise, brand and change it to make a better fit
- Deliver cost-effective, great value learning content that's proven to work.

Contact us today:
corporate.enquiries@pearson.com